D1742090

Planning Office Automation

Information Management Systems

**J A T Pritchard
and I Cole**

PUBLISHED BY NCC PUBLICATIONS

British Library Cataloguing in Publication Data

Pritchard, J. A. T.
   Planning office automation – information
management systems.
   1. Information services
   I. Title   II. Cole, I.
   658.4'03   Z7914.M27

ISBN 0-85012-366-6

MANAGEMENT

INFORMATION MANAGEMENT

© THE NATIONAL COMPUTING CENTRE LIMITED, 1983

First published in 1983 by:

NCC Publications, The National Computing Centre Limited, Oxford Road, Manchester M1 7ED, England.

Typeset in 10pt Times Roman and printed by UPS Blackburn Limited, 76-80 Northgate, Blackburn, Lancashire.

ISBN 0-85012-366-6

Acknowledgements

This book results from a distillation of the experiences and opinions of many people including persons employed by suppliers of equipment and services, users in both private and public sectors, and trade unionists.

In particular, the authors wish to thank the following for their time and support:

Alcan (UK) Ltd, Ashington (W F Baxter)
Amoco Production Company, Tulsa, Oklahoma, USA (J G Steward)
Association of Professional, Executive, Clerical and Computer Staff (APEX), Manchester (M Robinson)
Banking, Insurance and Finance Union (BIFU), Edinburgh (T Gardner)
Barclays Bank Limited, Knutsford (L A Edmonds)
Boeing Computer Services Company, Seattle, Washington, USA (G A Burton, P J Calandra, B R Wilson)
B P International Ltd, London (N G Barton)
British Embassy, Tokyo, Japan (M D Rogers)
British Telecom (M J Norton)
Central Electricity Generating Board (CEGB), London (K Bowers)
Ciba-Geigy P & A Company Ltd, Manchester (G P Roberts)
Ciba-Geigy (UK) Ltd, Paisley (D Alderton)
Compower Ltd, Cannock (A Burns)
Datapoint Corporation, San Antonio, Texas, USA (G Cullen, W Finkel, D Gust, H Merreaux, T J Moldenhauer, G B Thurmond)
Edinburgh Regional Computing Centre, Edinburgh (W Aitken)
Heriot-Watt University, Edinburgh (D Godfrey)
Hitachi Ltd, Tokyo, Japan (H Inoue, A Tamura)
Imperial Group Ltd, Bristol (J G Ross)

Japan Business Machine Makers Association (JBMA), Tokyo, Japan (A Saitoh)

Japan Information Processing Development Centre (JIPDEC), Tokyo, Japan (Mr Yamamoto, T Kobayashi, Y Yamadri)

Lothian Regional Council, Edinburgh (R Pitcairn)

Johns-Manville Sales Corporation, Denver, Colorado, USA (D L Bittner)

Manchester Polytechnic, Manchester (A J Wood)

Matsushita Communication Industrial Co Ltd, Yokohama, Japan (S Nagai)

Matsushita Graphic Communication Systems Inc, Tokyo, Japan (Mr Futakuchi, N N Mori)

John Menzies Ltd, Edinburgh (C Harrison, R Rutherford)

Mitsubishi Research Institute Inc, Tokyo, Japan (K Nagata)

Nexos Office Systems Ltd, Bristol (C Ellis)

Nippon Telegraph & Telephone Public Corporation (NTT), Tokyo, Japan (K Isozaki, Mr Tamura)

Office Technology Limited, Salford (Julie Thompson)

Oxford Polytechnic, Oxford (N J Butler)

Pilkington Brothers Ltd, St Helens (Ann Stanley)

Plessey Office Systems Ltd, Nottingham (D J Leyland)

Refuge Assurance Co Ltd, Manchester (Mr Betteridge)

Royal Bank of Scotland Ltd, Edinburgh (M Cooper, A Jackson)

Scottish Gas, Edinburgh (G Boyne)

Sharp Corporation, Tokyo, Japan (I Terashi, M Yokoyama)

Toshiba Corporation Research & Development Centre, Kawasaki, Japan (H Amano, C Michio, N Shimomura)

Toshiba Corporation, Tokyo, Japan (K Fujita, K Kaburagi, T Okamoto, Dr Okuda, H Yamamoto)

University of Tokyo, Tokyo, Japan (Prof H Yamada)

The authors also wish to thank their NCC colleagues for their advice and support:

K C E Gee
Irene Handley
S G Price
P A Wilson.

The Centre acknowledges with thanks the support provided by the Electronics and Aviation Requirements Board (EARB) – formerly the Computers, Systems and Electronics Requirements Board (CSERB) – for the project from which this publication derives.

Preface

'The electronic office as a total integrated information system is very much a concept of the future, but evolution towards it is clearly evident today. This book deals with current developments . . . It is the intention that future work . . . will look at the design, implementation and operation of the electronic office' (extract from the Preface to *Introducing the Electronic Office,* see Bibliography, item 1.1).

The work from which that book derived set the scene for a follow-up programme – and in 1980 NCC commenced a programme of work supported by the Department of Industry through the Computers, Systems and Electronics Requirements Board (CSERB). The aim of this programme is to establish the present and future needs of user organisations in the UK and their degree of satisfaction with existing products and services in the office automation (OA) area, and to produce books and guidance to assist users.

Initially a user survey was carried out to identify what progress was being made in the areas of electronic message systems (EMS) and information management systems (IMS). In-depth structured interviews were held with twelve organisations who were selected because they were known to have experience in – or plans at an advanced stage to become involved in – relevant OA systems. The findings were contained in a report *The Report of a Survey of UK Users (1980)* (see Bibliography, item 1.2).

Subsequently, work began upon a project which produced a book which aims to provide readers with advice which will assist them to develop an OA strategy, with particular reference to electronic message systems. That book is *Planning Office Automation – Electronic Message*

Systems (see Bibliography, item 1.3). Mindful that EMS can be but a part of an organisation's complete OA activity, a related project has been carried out to investigate strategic issues and design considerations for IMS (as the other project did for EMS), and has produced this book. It is anticipated that readers will read these two companion volumes together.

Other projects have investigated, or will investigate, the evaluation and selection of EMS and IMS products and services, and their implementation and operation. Other books and reports which have already been produced through NCC's OA work programme include the report of three workshops held in Manchester, London and Edinburgh in 1981: *Information Management Systems— Strategic Issues and Design Considerations* (see Bibliography, item 1.4) and the guidelines books *Electronic Mail Systems, Facsimile Equipment, Viewdata Systems* and *Office System Printers* (see Bibliography, items 1.5, 1.6, 1.7 and 1.8) and the multi-client study report *Managers and the New Technology* (see Bibliography, item 1.9).

Contents

1 Introduction

BACKGROUND

The National Computing Centre (NCC) commenced a major programme of work in the office automation (OA) area during 1980. One of the activities which has been completed was an investigation of how organisations should prepare an OA strategy, and of relevant strategic issues and design considerations which should be addressed. This investigation was carried out in two parts and two books have been produced: *Planning Office Automation — Electronic Message Systems* (see Bibliography, item 1.3); and this book.

The material gathered for the first book reflects experience and thinking during 1980 and the early part of 1981 and continues to be relevant. However, the demise towards the end of 1981 of the National Enterprise Board (NEB) venture, Nexos Office Systems, and with it the Delta Office Controller project, removes – temporarily at any rate – one OA strategy option which looked on paper to merit attention.

Further material for the present book was gathered during 1981 and 1982. This was a period of change in the office environment. New products and services – based upon microprocessor chips, communications satellites, fibre optics, optical disks, voice store-and-forward, voice recognition and other new technology – are being developed in the USA, Japan, the UK and elsewhere. Some of these products and services have begun to be used in offices in the UK. There have been changes too in awareness and attitudes towards OA in the UK, and IT82 (see below) was launched to increase awareness and to develop positive attitudes towards OA. Change in offices will continue during 1983 and beyond – and not only in offices but also in:

— factories, eg robots and data collection systems;

— shops and stores, eg electronic point-of-sale (EPOS) equipment and electronic funds transfer (EFT) transactions;

— secondary schools, eg the Government scheme to install micro-computers: this scheme was extended by the 1982 Budget, to cover primary schools also;

— society, eg the Government scheme to set up Information Technology Centres (Itecs) at Notting Dale and elsewhere (extended to one hundred Centres by the 1982 Budget) to provide the young unemployed with IT skills, the Open University's Cyclops 'electronic blackboard' terminals, the BBC's computer literacy project launched on BBC1 in January 1982 based on the Acorn microcomputer (ordered by 500 schools and 12,000 members of the public before the launch), and domestic Prestel and teletext sets;

— public transport, eg ticket issuing/data collection machines in buses;

— heavy goods vehicles, eg tachometers and their use for collecting data for computer analysis;

— other walks of life, eg hospitals, defence systems.

In several of these areas, new technology is being used to automate – and therefore to speed up and to make less expensive – various information-related tasks. However, whilst there is nothing wrong in using new technology for these reasons, it is imperative that investment attitudes should change significantly in those organisations which wish to survive the transition to the Information Society. Information must be perceived as a resource and managed accordingly, using automated processes. This will ensure that people have better-quality information and more time for creative thinking, for making better decisions, for increasing sales or for improving service levels. Information and information management processes must be integrated to add value to raw information. In the electronic office this integration will be achieved by investing in new technology, but a strategy is essential if problems are to be overcome and major benefits are to be attained.

To set the background for this book, it is interesting to comment briefly upon a number of recent events – they are part of the environment in which UK organisations are planning an OA strategy, undertaking pilot trials, or beginning to move forward towards the fully-integrated electronic office and the information society.

The UK Conservative Government, with a general philosophy of non-intervention and privatisation, has enacted the British Telecommunications Act. This splits the existing Post Office, which had operated under the Post Office Act of 1969, into two parts – British Telecom (BT) with telecommunications responsibilities, and a second body called the Post Office (but different from the pre-1981 body of that name) with postal responsibilities. The 1981 Act also provides for the relaxation of the monopoly position which had existed previously: there will be greater freedom for suppliers to be licensed to provide third-party value-added network services (VANS) using the BT network (see the Department of Industry guidelines in Appendix A), and for non-BT supplied equipment to be connected to the network.

Discussions took place and were concluded for a private consortium to be licensed by the Department of Industry (DoI) to offer communications services on a competing network, Mercury, using communications channels laid alongside British Rail tracks and some microwave transmission, but not BT network circuits. 1981 was the first full year of operation of the Ministry for Information Technology. The Minister, Mr Kenneth Baker, announced that 1982 would be Information Technology Year (IT82), and provided funding of £600,000. A national policy and planning committee (the 1982 Committee), under the chairmanship of Mr Alan Benjamin, was supported by nine regional committees, which prepared local programmes of events – debates, exhibitions, seminars, competitions etc.

IT82 was a nationwide awareness campaign aimed at promoting a wider appreciation of the opportunities, benefits and challenges provided by information technology among the general public as well as those in business and public administration. For IT82, NCC organised six mobile exhibition vans to tour the country and demonstrate electronic office equipment – appearing at The Grand National at Aintree, at County Shows and at many other events. The 'micro-van' project was launched in January 1982 by the Prime Minister, Mrs Margaret Thatcher, during a visit to NCC. This followed the opening, in April 1981, of NCC's Microsystems Centre in London.

The DoI has allocated funding for pilot electronic offices to be set up in public bodies with the aim of convincing all organisations, public and private sector, that there are benefits in office automation. Figure 1.1 shows the position towards the end of 1982. Twenty organisations had been accepted as suppliers, and user organisations were matched to them; other supplier/user pairings were under consideration.

The Government agreed to support the European Space Agency's L-Sat telecommunications satellite project with an investment of £77 million. During the next decade communications satellites will become a key element in a nation's telecommunications infrastructure: any nation ignoring this technology will put at risk its international competiveness and influence.

Organisations will have small dishes – frequently built into the roof of their building – to give them access to a range of value-added information services for facsimile transmission, messaging, video conferencing, external database access and retrieval, etc. The United Nations has designated 1983 as WCY83 (World Communications Year). It will be organised by the International Telecommunications Union (ITU), a UN agency, and will seek to develop communications infrastructure and focus attention upon the need for co-ordination at a national level. The aim is to ensure that communications are used to increase economic, social and cultural development throughout the world.

BT's new and long-awaited public packet switched service PSS began full commercial operation in August 1981 (see Chapter 4). In November 1981 BT announced that from 1982 a new range of digital transmission services would be marketed under the name of X-Stream. These services are MegaStream, KiloStream, SwitchStream (NB PSS has been renamed the SwitchStream 1 service) and SatStream (see Chapter 4).

During 1981 BL Systems Ltd, based at Redditch, was granted a five-year licence by BT to supply the Comet electronic mailbox system as a third-party intra-organisation messaging service for text messages; the Comet system was developed by the USA company Computer Corporation of America (CCA) of Cambridge, Massachusetts. BT introduced an electronic mail service for its Prestel viewdata system; it also announced its own electronic mail service, using the Dialcom software from the USA, and its teletex text communication service – this latter service will be operational in 1983. The Post Office introduced its Electronic Post

UK supplier	Public sector user
1 IBM (UK)	Cambridgeshire County Council 8100 DISOSS/DOSF
2 Xionics	Information Technology Unit, Cabinet Office
3 Rediffusion Computers	Information Technology Division, Department of Industry
4 Plessey Office Systems Ltd	Nottinghamshire County Council
5 Office Technology Ltd	British Rail Engineering Ltd., Derby
6 ICL*	Science and Engineering Research Council (SERC)
7 Data Recall*	Science and Engineering Research Council (SERC)
8 Rank Xerox	Greater London Council Ethernet, Star, 860 WP, 820 PC
9 Racal Information Systems	BBC Personnel Department Racal 6000
10 Allied Business Systems	Brighton General Hospital
11 Hewlett Packard	BBC Breakfast TV, Lime Grove Studios, London
12 Honeywell	Strathclyde Regional Council, Glasgow Education and Policy and Resources Committees Honeywell OAS and OCR
13 Systime	National Economic Development Office
14 Aregon	British Gas HQ Excom
15 Philips Business Systems	Department of Transport
16 GEC	Export Credit Guarantee Department, London and Cardiff
17 Future Technology Systems Ltd	Leicestershire Constabulary Series 88
18 Digital Equipment Ltd	British Telecom Long Range and Strategic Studies Division (BT LRSSD), Cambridge Office Plus
19 Burroughs	CEGB HQ (London) and South West Region HQ (Bristol) OFIS 1
20 Logica VTS	Wales Gas, Cardiff Polynet

*schemes 6 and 7 are linked.

Figure 1.1   DoI-Funded Electronic Office Schemes

service in London and Manchester (these postal areas cover 30% of the UK's 22 million addresses) using computers and laser printers.

One of the most important UK events in 1981 was the turnround of investors and user confidence in ICL. Severe financial problems and an incomplete range of products brought the company to its knees, but it was saved from extinction; under the new managing director, Mr Robb Wilmot, ICL has worked out a strategy for survival. It can now call upon the products and technology of the major Japanese computer company Fujitsu; and its product range also includes the DRS 20 office microcomputer, CAFS (see Chapter 4), the PERQ graphics workstation for professionals, the ME29 business computer, the Bulletin viewdata system, a personal computer based on the Rair Black Box, and the N2200 word processor (following the demise of Nexos Office Systems). It also concluded an agreement with Canadian company Mitel for a digital computer-based telephone exchange to be called DNX 2000, and has the Microlan and Macrolan local area networks (LANs).

Two young British companies beginning to catch the eye, as they moved quickly and confidently into the office systems market, were Xionics and Office Technology Limited (OTL). The Xionics system has been installed at Scottish Gas headquarters in Edinburgh and in other organisations. Xionics workstations are attached to a ring network called a Xinet through connection points called Intelligent Sockets. A small cabinet called a Xibus performs ring control and data management functions. OTL introduced its Information Management Processor (I.M.P.) late in 1981, a year later than Xionics. I.M.P. has facilities built into the workstation (which is based on the Intel 8086 microprocessor chip) for the voice annotation of documents.

Meanwhile, in June 1982, another British company Plessey Office Systems Ltd of Beeston, Nottingham, announced details of its IBIS (Integrated Business Information System) office systems strategy which is based on its PDX private digital telephone exchange. The system will support integrated workstations and, using a customer's existing telephone twisted-pair wiring, digital information will be transmitted at speeds of 64K bit/s concurrently with voice traffic. Racal too is now making moves in the OA market.

AIM OF THE BOOK; ITS AUDIENCE

This book is a companion volume to *Planning Office Automation—Electronic Message Systems* (see Bibliography, item 1.3) which aims to help its readers to devise a practical and effective strategy for introducing OA in general and EMS in particular, it is assumed that readers of this book will already have read the earlier one. The present book makes reference to relevant information about the OA strategy planning process contained in the EMS book.

An OA strategy covers the three areas of:

— document preparation systems (DPS);

— electronic message systems (EMS);

— information management systems (IMS).

This book discusses the strategic issues and design considerations which are relevant to the IMS which an organisation might wish to include in its OA strategy.

It is intended that this book, like the EMS book, should be read by anyone who will be involved with OA strategy, but particularly by those personnel who are concerned with organising or carrying out a strategy study. Some organisations have taken the step of creating a department or unit to plan for the introduction into offices of sytems, workstations and other equipment based upon microprocessors, optical disks, optical character recognition (OCR), communications satellites, voice recognition, facsimile, contents addressable file storage, digital transmission,

---

Managers, deputy managers and members of the following departments:

— administration;

— telecommunications;

— management services;

— office systems (or office services);

— data processing;

— corporate planning and research;

— office automation (or office technology);

Consultants;

Trades union officials.

Figure 1.2 The Audience for this Book

digital PABXs and other advanced technology. They have created positions such as Manager of Office Automation. An approach taken by other
organisations is to form working groups or committees for this purpose.
Figure 1.2 lists the personnel whose terms of reference should include
some involvement with OA strategic planning; it is for this audience that
the present book is primarily intended.

Subsequent chapters discuss:

— the role of the information resource in organisations;

— the OA strategic planning process;

— the classification of information into various categories and relev-
    ant IMS technology and products;

— strategic issues relevant to IMS strategy planning;

— design considerations relevant to IMS strategy planning;

— relevant future developments.

UNDERSTANDING THE BENEFITS OF OFFICE AUTOMATION

There is now a large amount of UK experience in the use of word
processors, although there are still far too many organisations who have
not yet taken even this small step towards the electronic office. NCC
introduced word processing into its typing pool at the beginning of 1977
with two Wordplex machines (NB it is always wise to have at least two
because it is most unlikely that both will be non-operational at the same
time). Later a third and then a fourth machine were brought in as authors
appreciated the advantages to themselves (and to the typists) of commit-
ting the following types of work to a word processor rather than to an
electric typewriter:

— books, reports, manuals and other documents which pass through
    an iterative drafting process;

— letters and contracts which draw on standard paragraphs;

— lists of names and addresses of people and articles, things to do
    (the tickler file), itineraries, and other documents which need to
    be updated frequently (but maintained in an alphabetical or some
    other structured order).

Word processing is one entry point – quite a good one, but there are others – onto the migration path which leads to the electronic office and to corporate survival into the 1990s. NCC introduced word processing as an electronic aid to make the document preparation function more efficient by taking advantage of the new technology at its state of advancement current at that time. This expenditure was justified by the cost savings and other benefits which it was expected to bring – and which were subsequently shown to have been achieved.

Word processing investment justification decisions were being made from 1977 in the UK on the (valid) basis that there would be net cost savings and productivity gains in the documentation preparation function, rather than on the basis that an organisation had a strategy for OA and that word processing was the first step in the implementation of that strategy. Now word processing brings productivity gains to: typists particularly, because they spend such a high proportion of their relatively low-paid time upon the document preparation function; authors to some extent, because it is necessary for them to check corrections only and not complete retypes; and secretaries only to a limited degree, because they spend only 20% to 30% or thereabouts of their time on the document preparation function. Consequently an attitude has developed among too many people in decision-making positions in UK organisations to the effect that OA technology should be directed at improving the productivity of typists, secretaries and other support staff in the office environment. Until quite recently it did not matter too much because word processing was more or less the only cost-effective OA tool that suppliers had to offer – but great technological strides have changed this situation dramatically in the early 1980s and will continue to do so.

New OA products and systems are beginning to appear and will, within a year or two, flood onto the market. In large part these are aimed at making the relatively highly-paid people within an organisation more effective and more productive. Until recently OA investment has been largely aimed at automating the highly structured tasks of the lower-paid office worker who is employed to perform such tasks as:

— typing;

— filing;

— carrying bits of paper;

— photocopying;

—   shorthand dictation;

—   the playing by a personal secretary of 'telephone tag' with an
    opposite number in another organisation (so that their superiors
    do not have to waste their time doing the same).

Increasingly these tasks can be assisted by automation or even avoided
altogether. Indeed it has been estimated that in 1979 $50 billion was
spent in the USA on information resources for clerical and typing workers, but only $24 billion was spent on managers and professionals (see
Bibliography, item 1.10).

Productivity (eg through using machines to do more cheaply the work
of people) and *effectiveness* are not necessarily the same thing; an example in Chapter 5 illustrates the difference between using added value (ie
increased effectiveness) rather than cost savings (ie increased productivity) as the criterion for the justification of a viewdata system. 'Productivity' is not too difficult to define and to measure in a manufacturing
environment, whereas in an office environment it is not easy to define, let
alone measure. In a factory, productivity is output produced per unit of
input; in financial terms it is, perhaps, the output per unit cost, ie the
quantity of output divided by the costs of production. Effectiveness is,
perhaps, the contribution towards profits per unit of output (or per £1 of
production costs).

There is a danger that OA will be perceived as simply automating
existing practices (ie as raising office productivity) and that OA strategy
planning and investment will be based upon this narrow perception. What
is necessary is for an organisation to try to understand what its office
workers are trying to achieve rather than to identify and to automate
those tasks or activities which are the ways in which existing processes are
carried out. An example will illustrate what we are trying to say.

Professionals frequently need to read articles to keep up-to-date, and
to refer back to these articles when preparing presentations and writing
reports. Consequently a secretary or clerical assistant may be requested
to make, say, ten copies of a seven-page article and distribute the ten sets
of collated photocopied papers to the ten different professionals. The
assistant may also be asked to make eight copies of a four-page article, to
make five copies of a ten-page article, and finally to service a fourth
request for five copies of a twelve-page article. These tasks may have to
be completed in the same afternoon. It is also necessary to fill in the

associated paperwork to allow the work to be monitored so that the unit costs for the service to internal departments can be updated and so that the costs for the provision of the service can be calculated to facilitate interdepartmental paper transfers of money.

One problem is that the photocopying machine may not automatically collate, although it can do multiple copies. It cannot reduce a large page size to A4 size and it requires its operator to determine the best setting of the brightness control for each of the four different original journals. A manager with a 'quill pen' attitude approaches this problem by looking at microprocessor-controlled photocopying machines which are reliable, quick and convenient to use, then carrying out a cost-benefit analysis, and finally installing the one which emerges as the best buy from the evaluation and selection process. In other words, an inherently inefficient process is simply being automated.

This approach is no longer appropriate for organisations wishing to survive and thrive in the information society. *Ad hoc* investment decisions must give way to a corporate OA strategy which recognises information as a resource and seeks to integrate the various information management processes.

In the case of the photocopier user in our example, what should be done? First, there has to be a recognition that what the photocopier user is doing is only a means to an end; it is not an end in itself. This distinction is crucial to planning an OA strategy, but it is often not understood.

Second, there has to be a recognition that the 'end', which is giving rise to this activity, is the expressed wish of professionals to collect photocopies of articles which they need now or which they may need to refer to at one or more times in the future. Many professionals have come to work in this way, to hoard paper inside personal filing systems, often resulting in relevant information being buried by vast quantities of irrelevant material.

Third, there has to be a recognition that what managerial, professional and technical staff really need is a quick and convenient means of determining whether any relevant documents exist and of retrieving those they require. The Amoco approach to electronic filing provides professionals with a different and better way of working (see Chapter 6). There, after nearly four years of electronic office working, 80,000 documents were filed in the computer system. Some of the indexed documents are stored on-line and can be displayed on the user's terminal. Others are held in a centralised paper-filing system and can be borrowed and returned within a certain time. A document only needs to be photocopied if a hard copy is needed to be taken away, or to be annotated, or if the user needs to work with the document for a long time. Consequently the need for photocopying is significantly reduced, and has in practice declined very considerably. The emphasis has changed from improving the photocopying service to 'resystematising' office procedures so that the need for the photocopying activity is significantly reduced.

Fourth, there has to be a recognition that an OA strategy is needed and that it must take account of all the needs of all the office workers. In this context it is necessary:

— to allow staff to make better-informed decisions by providing them with quick and easy-to-use means of access to up-to-date, relevant information;

— to facilitate more effective communication between persons: for example, electronic mail and other text messaging systems, teletex, electronic voice messaging systems;

— improving within-organisation information dissemination: for example, by a private viewdata system.

Productivity can be increased by reducing the amount of keyboarding. This can be achieved partly by designing office systems so that, after information has been keyed in once, the same information does not have to be keyed in again, and partly by designing office systems so that the keying can be avoided altogether: OCR or voice recognition can be used. Productivity can also be increased by:

— reducing the amount of paper handling and other labour-intensive tasks, particularly those associated with messaging and filing;

— automating document preparation, messaging and information management tasks;

— pushing work downwards so that it is carried out by the lowest-paid job grade which is competent to handle it (see Figure 1.3).

OA, however, provides great opportunities for increasing not only productivity but also effectiveness. Of the three aspects of OA, DPS are concerned particularly with increasing productivity, eg word processing,

Simplify office procedures to reduce the total number of keyboarding, paper handling and other labour-intensive tasks through eliminating some and avoiding others.

Use word processors, personal workstations with at least local site communications facilities and other electronic office equipments to automate the residual keyboarding, messaging, filing and other office activities following the simplification of office procedures.

Delegate and reassign work to lower-paid job grades (eg managers to professionals and administrative secretaries, professionals to administrative secretaries and administrative support centres, administrative secretaries to junior administrative support centre personnel) to create opportunity hours at as high a level of job grade as possible.

Figure 1.3   Ways of Increasing Office Productivity

while EMS and IMS are concerned with both productivity and effectiveness. EMS can raise productivity by allowing people to send text messages, and other forms of information, to each other in a way which eliminates labour-intensive, and therefore costly, paper-based stages of the message transfer process. Since people can send electronic messages quickly and conveniently to each other, they will now be able to send messages which hitherto it would have been impractical or too much trouble to send but which nevertheless are worthwhile sending. This increased effectiveness of communication means that people become more effective in their work and decision making because they are:

— better informed;

— better able to control projects;

— better able to respond to events.

On the other hand many message flows can be eliminated such as the 'telephone-tag' type of telephone message which:

— is responsible for so much unproductive use of manpower in offices;

— causes frustration;

— causes telephone extensions to be engaged and people to be unnecessarily inaccessible;

— causes inroads into the time, concentration and capacity for creative work of the participants in the 'telephone-tag' activities;

— incurs BT line charges (in the case of calls out of the message
originator's building).

IMS can raise productivity because people have easier access to information, and – because the information is more up-to-date, complete and
relevant – people can be more effective too.

At The National Computing Centre, a Nestar Cluster/One local area
network (LAN) was installed by Zynar in September 1981. The manager,
divisional secretary and ten professionals of the Office and Communications Systems Division all have their own Apple II microcomputer. These
workstations are connected by a ribbon cable to a 33 Mbyte fileserver and
draft quality printer located in the computer operations room, and to a
letter quality printer in the secretary's office. The reasons for putting in
this local network were:

— to enable the NCC division which is responsible for helping users
to introduce and benefit from OA – by writing books, reports and
articles, holding workshops, carrying out public speaking engage-
ments, participating in the work of standards-making bodies, etc –
to gain hands-on experience of new office technology;

— to serve as a pilot experiment to provide evidence on whether or
not local networking concepts should be introduced more widely
in NCC;

— to gain the benefits which local networking is claimed to bring.

The electronic office facilities which are available in this LAN can be
summarised as:

— electronic mail (EMS)

— text creation using the Pascal Editor (DPS)

— text creation using the Wordstar word processing software (DPS)

— electronic filing (personal files) (IMS)

— electronic filing (shared access (read only) divisional files created
by the divisional secretary and holding divisional administrative
information) (IMS)

— electronic filing (project files created by professionals with shared access by colleagues on a read only basis, or on a read and write basis, as appropriate (IMS).

The first of these facilities is EMS, enabling useful messages to be sent which would not have been because:

— the effort of organising a typed memorandum and /or the delay involved in delivering it to the recipients would be too great;

— the sender of an internal telephone message did not want to be drawn into a game of telephone tag;

— the sender did not want to interrupt the recipient during a meeting or whilst engaged in creative thinking;

— the sender knew that the recipient was away.

Electronic mail also enables messages to be copied, forwarded, filed for future reference and answered quickly and conveniently. This facility has enabled all members of the division to gain a better appreciation of what others are doing and of their attitudes towards current issues, and therefore for all to be more effective in their line management, forward planning, project control, project development, administrative support and other work. The facility has also been used successfully for the in-depth examination of selected topics, and as a frustration vent. So here is evidence of an EMS making office workers more effective.

The second and third facilities are DPS. All users are able to create, and edit text in their personal and project files using the Pascal Editor – otherwise they would be limited to using electronic mail and to reading filed information created by others and, with such a limited commitment to this electronic office system, would derive little benefit. The divisional secretary derives considerable benefit from the word processing facility and the letter quality printer, the use of which is under her control. Some use of this facility is made by her colleagues but a limitation is that any output from the letter quality printer requires that the divisional secretary shall not concurrently use her Apple II workstation. Wordstar files to be printed require that the secretary is given specific detailed information, but Pascal files to be printed can be automatically queued; this latter situation is less inconvenient for the secretary, but either situation is somewhat inconvenient for the professional. This limitation is not too severe as the Pascal Editor is adequate for much of the professional's text creation requirements and the draft quality printer can be used to print text created by Wordstar unless the whole point of using Wordstar was to create a well-formatted document for letter quality print-out.

The fourth, fifth and sixth facilities are IMS – the topic being examined in this book. This is probably the area where the greatest pay-off exists in the electronic office in the long-term, but also the area which is the most difficult to plan for in such a way that the full benefits are achieved. At present, in offices everywhere, masses and masses of paper-based information, some useful, some useless, are stored or stuffed away. Potential users are unlikely:

— to know all the information held;

— to know where it is;

— to be satisfied with the procedures for adding new information, for searching for and retrieving information from current and archived paper files, for transferring information from current to archived files, or for deleting information from current and archived files.

Some organisations have created administrative support centres (ASCs) and centralised filing systems (paper files or a mixture of electronic and paper filing with a computer-based indexing and retrieval system for all electronic and paper documents). Even when technology is cost-effective in storing all documents electronically in on-line storage and when any user can immediately access, retrieve and display at a workstation any particular electronic document of interest wherever in the world it is stored, there still remains a big problem. It is this – a user generally does not know which particular documents are wanted; instead the user wants to know whether there are any documents relevant to the enquiry that are worth spending time browsing through. This will be a key issue in the design of IMS in the electronic office and a key factor in determining whether users will in fact use the workstation sitting in front of them. As electronic filing, shared-access departmental and corporate files, and external public data bases grow – as they will – it is essential that keyword indexing and other document access/retrieval methods are quick and convenient to use and provide users with relevant documents; users must not be swamped with masses of out-of-date or irrelevant documents along with the up-to-date and relevant ones.

The sharing of filed information has allowed members of the division to be better informed about the progress of work which colleagues are carrying out, and to be of assistance to each other. For instance, it is a simple matter to keep an up-to-date file of work completed and in progress, to print a copy and give it to visitors or to people who enquire by letter or telephone. Nevertheless, electronic filing is an area which has important system design and security implications when there are many users and many departments or communities of users.

The subject of OA benefits (ie cost savings and added value) is so important that NCC has undertaken a project to discuss with users what benefits they have achieved from private viewdata systems, local area networks, advanced word processing systems and other OA systems of which there is by now quite an amount of practical experience in a few UK organisations. The findings are reported in the book *Office Technology Benefits* (see Bibliography, item 1.11).

OA systems can save manpower by allowing some tasks to be avoided and by allowing others to be completed with less human involvement. Paper costs, filing cabinet costs, postage and telephone costs, etc, can be reduced. Cost savings are important for they help an organisation to raise its productivity and to remain competitive by offering its products and services at a reasonable price vis-a-vis those of its rivals. But no less important are the added value benefits of OA systems. People can be more effective, more responsive to inquiries from customers. For instance a typist at a word processor might be able to include, within a letter or report, information (facts, figures, histograms, etc) retrieved from Prestel or a private viewdata system to support a point.

2 The Role and Management of Information

This chapter seeks to make the reader aware of the importance of perceiving information, in all of its forms, as a resource, and of the importance of handling (ie managing) this resource effectively.

INFORMATION AS A RESOURCE

A major factor limiting the effectiveness of industry is the difficulty in handling the increasing amount of information needed to support competitive levels of production. The advent of electronic office technology has provided, and will continue to provide, the means to enhance the management of information across a broad spectrum of office environments, allowing people a greater control over their tasks.

Information management is also necessary in terms of economic factors. First, if an organisation does not remain competitive, because employees do not handle information as effectively as do competitors, then trade and revenue will be lost. Second, the acquisition of information costs money; manpower is required to access or generate information internally; also, information received from third-party sources has to be paid for, and usually incurs telecommunications costs. Both of these factors have contributed to a situation where information is regarded as an economic resource, and where there is a significant need for effective information management.

A US report (*Records and Paperwork Management in the Federal Government: Two Decades of Recommendations*) found that in the mid-1950s there were more than 25 billion cubic feet of government records in existence, with the annual costs of records management at that time to the US government estimated to be $4 billion. More recent studies have found that more than one-third of total office costs involve the preparation, duplication, handling and storage of paper. US industry holds over 265 billion documents in storage, and the US federal government even more (see Bibliography, item 2.1).

Without adopting OA, many organisations are unlikely to survive beyond the 1980s. The cost of labour-intensive paper-based information handling procedures will harm them economically and the slowness of retrieving information will impair the quality of their response to events, inquiries, etc, and make them uncompetitive.

Twenty years ago, an efficient secretary was sufficient to turn a reasonably competent manager into quite an effective one, but this is no longer true today in circumstances where:

— information flows have grown greatly;

— the effective office worker is one who can identify specific information needs and quickly access the appropriate information (the person who merely reacts to information flows will not work effectively).

The traditional personal secretary will no longer be able to cope. Administrative support centres (ASCs) and centralised paper filing systems constitute the environment into which the new office systems should be introduced. Only in this way can the full benefits be achieved, and the criticism that one is 'automating the existing mess' be avoided.

In the conventional office, information flows in and is dealt with on arrival. In the electronic office, the nature of information flows will change. Information will be filed electronically in files which can be accessed at any time by anyone who has access rights. People will receive electronic mail notifying them of the existence of information in electronic filing systems, instead of receiving photocopies of the actual information, and so can be more selective in accordance with their information requirements. In the conventional office:

— information arrives which we do not want or need;

— useful information sometimes arrives when we do not need it;

— information disappears (borrowed, stolen, misfiled, etc);

— filed information cannot be retrieved when it is urgently needed (because the manager's secretary is absent, because the professional's filing system is badly structured, or because the person who filed it cannot remember where it is filed).

In the electronic office, by contrast, information is retrieved by users when they require it, so the problem of useless information arriving on someone's desk is eliminated: no information arrives unless it has been demanded. This also eliminates the problem of useful information arriving on someone's desk at an inopportune time. Moreover, with adequate security provisions, electronic information cannot disappear without trace: when someone requests a copy, the stored original remains intact.

Finally the problem of not being able to find information when it is urgently required is almost, but not quite entirely, eliminated. Where a user has a user-friendly interface to aid the search for electronically-filed information, one problem may be the way in which information is filed: it can be difficult to design filing guidelines which will enable all users to retrieve information easily. People have personal preferences for filing paper documents and will likewise have preferences for electronic filing structures. Each user will organise personal electronic files to suit particular retrieval methods. In the electronic office, files will be subject to shared access and some users may not find some filing structures to their liking. As an example many users have complained of the searching problems encountered in using Prestel. It is easy to learn how to use Prestel, but it can be cumbersome to use it to extract information because:

— there is a lack of page format standards;

— users get lost in the tree structure or take too long (or even fail) to find the required pages;

— categories of pages are labelled inconsistently and often have a fuzzy connection with the information contained therein.

In terms of advantage, electronic filing and shared access to information in electronic files:

— facilitate and stimulate creative thinking (this is the most important advantage);

— avoid the wasteful and frustrating duplication of effort (currently encountered because there is a lack of knowledge about available information and its location), by ensuring that information once captured in electronic form can be retrieved and reused;

— provide time and cost savings in searching for and retrieving information (eg photocopying is eliminated).

Much information needed by managers and professionals is held externally in public reference libraries, in government department offices and in town halls. Visitors can browse through books, reports and documents and gather a mass of relevant information or have specific questions answered on the telephone or by letter or telex. But this takes time and is not instantaneous. Consequently on-line information services have been established and their use can be expected to grow. This type of information, external information, is dicussed in Chapter 4.

All office workers know what a vast amount of information can arise in the course of a day: reports, journals, questionnaires, management notices, union notices, sports and social club notices, typed drafts and graphical artwork for checking, product brochures from suppliers, etc. Some of these documents have to be filed, some have to be photocopied, some have to be annotated and sent elsewhere, and some can be thrown away. Some information comes in on the telephone, some via a visitor or colleague. This information frequently has to be noted for future reference by writing down a summary of it upon paper, just as incoming documents often also have to be scanned and a summary written down. Office workers are constantly faced with making decisions about how to use their time:

— should they scan their information heaps?

— should they process, file and otherwise dispose of their information heaps?

— should they carry on with the management function, project development work, administrative support work, typing, etc, which is what they are primarily employed to do?

Senior office workers have often been able to argue that their personal secretary is essential. Without this support, he would go under – submerged by paper blizzards, trapped in the convolutions of telephone-tag mazes, or multi-scheduled to attend simultaneous meetings. Professionals, on the other hand, do not generally receive any significant degree of support from secretarial staff, but neither do they have to cope with the administration of this resource (eg finding a replacement when the secretary is away or leaves); nor are they unable to access their paper-based filing systems as managers often are in the absence of secretaries.

This description makes information appear to be as much a liability as an asset. In far too many offices, this is the reality. At present, office workers have little control over what information they receive, or when they receive it. They often have difficulty in managing their own information and in discovering what information is held by others in their organisation or in public filing systems.

THE INFORMATION MANAGER

The management of a multinational corporation's far-flung resources and assets is a formidable and information-intensive task. Those professionals responsible for the creation of wealth in the organisation cannot function effectively without reliable and up-to-date information. It is evident, therefore, that information is as much a corporate resource as the more traditional capital investments, such as new plant. Futhermore, substantial corporate investment in systems for the management of information will be necessary to ensure an organisation's future survival against competitors. In today's modern organisation the management of information and data is of paramount importance.

An *information manager* could be asked to ensure that information management systems are implemented and used in a way conducive to the efficient and effective running of the organisation. The appointment of such a person would alleviate one of the problems inherent in planning for information management systems: namely, to whom do you allocate responsibility for the various stages in this process?

The job will demand various imaginative and creative talents, and it should not be assumed that every computer centre manager will rise to the challenge. It is also doubtful (F. W. Horton, Bibliography, item 2.3) 'that the librarian, the information centre chief, the reports control officer, the records manager, the chief statistician, the chief of the printing branch, or even the trained information scientist, will be able to rise to the challenge without additional experience and training'. The modern information manager needs to have a range of skills. One way of viewing the complexity and specialisation of the information manager's job is by reviewing the list of job specifications, in his nominal area, which the American Society for Information Science periodically publishes (see Bibliography, item 2.4).

In the past, computer storage and retrieval of information has been restricted mainly to data processing systems. However, today there is a progressive emphasis upon the more informal and less proceduralised requirements of information management found in the office environment. Information managers should reflect this changing context. Certainly they should embrace the convergence of office technology, computer science, information science, and telecommunications.

The responsibilities of the corporate information manager would, according to Horton, be to:

— 'provide overall co-ordination of company-wide efforts to improve the planning, development, and operation of corporate and departmental information systems;

— develop policies and technical guidance to assist individual operating departments and corporate headquarters in the continuing management of their information systems activities and in implementing responsibilities outlined in the overall company information management programme;

— identify and initiate improved ways of achieving compatibility between information systems and different departments, through such programmes as standard definitions and terms for commonly-used data elements and codes;

— provide for the establishment and operation of one or more company information centres. As a first step, develop and maintain a comprehensive inventory of departmental and corporate information systems. This inventory will service all authorised users by providing them, upon request, with information on the existence, name, location, purpose, content, and other data concerning both departmental and corporate information systems, as well as the substantive data content of such sytems;

— provide for the establishment of training programmes to encourage and enable departments to accomplish more effectively the goals and objectives of their programmes and acquire the necessary technical and managerial know-how and skills;

— provide technical advice and assistance to departments in evaluating, modifying, and improving existing systems and information management practices and in developing new systems;

— prepare periodic, company-wide information systems improvement reports on both the short- and long-term information needs of the company as a whole, as well as the needs of the individual departments, in the management and co-ordination of information systems;

— make lead departmental assignments for the development of additional company-wide information systems and for the continued operation of existing corporate and departmental information systems.'

Interfaces between the company's central information manager and the heads of individual departments and divisions are also important. The central information manager will be expected to:

— assist the heads of individual departments and divisions to establish departmental information policies consistent with the general information policies of the corporation as a whole. For example, these might include the interchange of substantive data and information systems knowledge and technology and the development and utilisation of company-wide information systems that are multi-purpose of character and use, in lieu of developing a myriad number of single-purpose information systems;

— assist departmental heads in establishing a comprehensive department-wide information programme to provide for the orderly acquisition, enhancement, retention and delivery of information resources within the department – an example of this activity might be the establishment of two- to five-year plans for the development of departmental information systems;

— assist departmental heads in the development of procedures and controls to ensure adequate justification, documentation, review and approval of proposed new information systems or the modification of existing systems. A part of this process would be to ensure that alternate approaches were fully explored to satisfy the achievement of expected goals and objectives by the information systems.

DECISION-MAKING AND PROBLEM-SOLVING

We have discussed how the present information explosion, and the costs involved in acquiring, storing, and retrieving relevant information, have resulted in information being increasingly regarded as a financial resource. However, in order to understand fully the implications of effective information management it is useful to examine the role that information plays in decision-making/problem-solving.

Making a decision involves using information to assess the present state of a particular decision-making environment, the desired state of that environment, and the possible courses of action which are necessary to turn the former state into the latter. In order to make an appropriate decision the information used must be relevant, valid, accurate, up-to-date and comprehensive.

There are a number of decision points in problem-solving:

— identify the problem – this is the most important step in any problem-solving strategy: if a problem (or objective) is not properly identified none of the remaining steps or decision points will occur and the true nature of the problem (or objective) will remain unkown;

— define the problem – it is not enough to identify a problem, it must be defined before it can be fully understood and subsequent action can be taken to resolve it;

— assess the problem – before appropriate steps can be applied to solve a problem, its magnitude, character and consequences must be assessed; this will prevent uneconomical or ineffective solutions;

— define the information needed – following the previous steps, there is usually a need for more information to provide a better understanding as well as a conceptual basis for the design and development of appropriate alternative solutions to the problem. The aim is to define that information which is relevant to the problem (or objective); this in turn is regulated by the problem assessment step, which, if incorrect, can result in too much or too little information;

— identify the sources of information – information can be directly obtained from some form of information storage and retrieval system, or as a result of interaction with colleagues. Information can also be acquired through the interpretation of data; there are a number of stages:

    — define the data;

- identify data sources;

- collect the data;

- validate and verify collected data;

- assimilate, correlate, interpret, and evaluate data;

- integrate information into knowledge structure – information may have instrinsic or potential value. However, its true value is realised only when it removes uncertainty and contributes to human understanding and knowledge. This requires that information is effectively applied to the resolution of problems and the achievement of objectives, with a view to testing its relevance to and increasing knowledge of those problems. Misinformation can result in counter-productivity, and can increase the ineffectiveness of problem solvers;

- apply the knowledge – knowledge is applied to understand better the problem or objective, and possibly to redefine it with greater precision and accuracy, and iterate the process again up to this point;

- assess solution consequences – this stage provides feedback as to the appropriateness of the preceding stages in providing practical solutions to the identified problem (there should also be feedback at each intermediate stage);

- apply the solution – the outcome of the previous decisions should be the application of solutions appropriate to problem resolution. This will only occur if the information used at each stage is optimum with regard to requirements.

It is evident from our cursory look at the problem-solving process that appropriate information is necessary at each of the stages if optimum solutions are to be found. In turn, the availability of appropriate information is dependent upon effective information management. However, in planning for information management systems, especially as tools to aid decision-making, fundamental questions need to be asked. For example, who is using the information and why?

An information management system gives us a better chance of getting the right information and data to the right people at the right times. This kind of support can add another dimension of accuracy to decision-making, and will make its greatest cost/benefit impact in the area of management. For instance, a sales manager could project orders based on history kept in an archive file in the DP centre, or elsewhere: sitting at a workstation, a manager might view graphic or numerical representations of sales information, vary the results in 'what if' mode, and calculate projections under a variety of conditions.

3 Strategic Planning Considerations

This chapter discusses the OA strategic planning process, as opposed to the strategic issues and design considerations which the OA strategic plan should address (discussed in Chapters 5 and 6). The reader's attention is also drawn to Chapter 2, 'Preparing the Strategy Study', in *Planning Office Automation – Electronic Message Systems* (see Bibliography, item 1.3).

Without strategic planning, individual departments will probably install components of the electronic office to solve existing problems and bring short-term benefits, but will take too little account of company-wide needs. Strategic planning is necessary to prevent it being difficult, costly or impossible to integrate the variety of document-preparation, messaging and information management processes of a multitude of single-function and multifunction workstations.

Both the strategic planning and the plan which emerges from it are important. OA planners in user organisations have declared that the planning process itself is more important for, while the plan shows the direction in which the organisation is heading at any moment (ie the specific steps along the migration path leading towards the fully integrated electronic office), the planning process should cause the organisation to:

— remain flexible and able to change direction (this is important because technology is changing so fast);

— review on a continual basis its needs, experience gained from existing OA systems within the organisation (experimental pilot systems and permanent operational systems), and the costs, availability and performance of new and existing OA products and services in the marketplace;

41

— monitor and update its OA strategic plan on an on-going basis.

OA will:

— affect all office workers, by eliminating some jobs altogether and altering the nature of others;

— require, in many organisations, a very significant degree of resystematisation of office procedures, redeployment and retraining;

— require immense investment (which will lead to immense savings and benefits) in workstations, the communications infrastructure, and retraining;

— require investment decisions which will be complex and have far-reaching consequences.

Therefore the strategic planning process must:

— have the right terms of reference;

— be carried out by the right persons;

— ask the right questions and gather the right information;

— come to the right conclusions;

— produce plans which are capable of implementation.

OBJECTIVES

Any strategic plan should seek to answer the questions 'What?' and 'When?', because it should indicate what types of OA system an organisation needs and provide an investment strategy (or a number of alternatives) for its board, council, policy committee or other decision-making units to deliberate about, as well as a phased implementation schedule. In reaching answers to these questions, however, the questions 'Why?' and 'How?' also need to be addressed so that the investment decisions can be identified and so that, when workstations arrive on desks or shared resources arrive in information centres and administrative support centres, users will know what they are for, know how to use them and will use them (not always the case at present!).

The first question to ask, then, is 'Why?':

— why do we need to use new technology in offices at all?

— why do we need to do this or that (eg regroup personal secretaries into secretariats, centralise all paper-based filing on departmental and/or corporate lines and withdraw paper files from personal filing cabinets, install an electronic document filing system using an optical disk with laser scanner and laser printer, install an internal private viewdata system, etc)?

— why can we not leave things as they are or wait until better OA systems become available, as they undoubtedly will, which will be more cost-effective, easier to use, compatible with other systems, and multi-functional?

The 'Why?' questions must make the strategic planners look at:

— the organisation's existing office practices;

— the existing activity analysis schedules of typical senior managers, line managers, professionals, secretaries, typists, mail clerks and other categories of office personnel;

> (NB these first two points are important because it is necessary to identify the 'existing mess', so that the benefits which can be expected from OA systems can be estimated, quantitatively and qualitatively and so that the degree and nature of change within the organisation can be assessed and planned for; it is most important to avoid simply acquiring new technology because it is fashionable to do so and using it solely to 'automate the existing mess'.)

— the document preparation, messaging and information management *needs,* rather than the *activities,* of managers, professionals, salesmen and other decision makers and wealth-creators.

The second question to ask is 'What?':

— what communications infrastructure is needed to support the electronic message systems, and the information flows of the information management systems?

— what types of OA system are required (ie what types of multifunction workstation do different categories of individual office worker require and what shared-use equipment is required)?

— what are the benefits and cost savings, and what costs (of workstations, communications equipment, network, software, training, etc) are involved – and what are the costs and consequences of not investing in OA systems?

— what are our priorities?

'What?' questions cause the strategic planners to be specific about the proposals that they are recommending for investment and implementation approval.

The third question to ask is 'When?':

— when should investment and implementation take place?

This question requires that the financial aspects of OA are examined in detail. For each year of the period covered by the strategic plan, actual – and present worth – expenditure on OA, cost savings and financial benefits such as increased sales turnover must be estimated, so that the cash flow position is kept under control.

Senior management must decide to what extent expenditure is met by cost savings, additional revenue, reserves, borrowing and any government and/or EEC grants which may be available. High interest rates on borrowed money, redundancy payments, and declining markets in the UK and abroad do not make it easy for private companies to incur expenditure on new technology.

On the other hand, local government authorities are faced with government constraints on expenditure which annually become more and more difficult to comprehend and to administer. This makes it difficult but even more necessary to plan ahead in order to obtain the benefits of a well-prepared strategy implemented over a period of from, say, five to seven years. In hard times, however, organisations make great efforts to increase productivity and to be better prepared to prosper when the hard times end. In good times, when organisations can afford to invest, there is not the same urge to do so.

In either case, good management and strategic planning are essential. An implementation schedule is necessary not only for financial reasons but also to allow time for the planning and execution of pre-implementation changes such as:

— rewiring of offices and buildings;

— obtaining BT lines and modems;

— mounting an internal publicity campaign to raise employees' awareness of electronic office technology and systems;

— consulting and agreeing with the unions on regrading, redeployment and redundancy (if any).

The fourth question to ask is 'How?':

— how should office organisation structures and practices be changed (if at all) to ensure that users will derive the planned-for benefits and cease spending portions of their time inefficiently and ineffectively?

This question will cause the strategic planners to heed any New Technology Agreement which the organisation has entered into with a trades union, to identify retraining requirements and to see that these are fulfilled, and to redeploy, as appropriate, secretaries, typists, clerks and other support staff who will be needed in the electronic office.

PROCEDURES

To set up a strategy study it is necessary to:

— define terms of reference for the study and gain authorisation;

— allocate responsibilities for the study;

— decide on the tasks and timescales for the study;

— decide what level of employee involvement in the study should be sought.

The reader is referred to Chapter 2, 'Preparing the Strategy Study', of *Planning Office Automation – Electronic Message Systems* (see Bibliography, item 1.3) for further information and advice.

To prepare an OA strategy it is necessary to collect information about the business and currently-available technology, and then to make decisions based on that information. Some of the needed information may already be available. To determine other information you may have to mount specific studies. Most people do not recommend large detailed studies because:

— they take too long;

— the information so obtained is rarely very much more accurate than a quick rough-and-ready study;

— the current environment is probably not a good guide to the future.

For these reasons we advise you keep your study relatively quick and simple and make do with approximate answers.

There are seven categories of information which will be useful in devising an OA strategy with particular emphasis on IMS:

— *the business*. The objectives of the business; what it does; its official policies; what its plans are;

— *the organisation structure*. The functional responsibilities of groups and individuals; the reporting structure; geographical locations of groups and individuals; future changes in any of these;

— *the staff*. Categories of employees; number of employees in each category; characteristics of each category; groupings; industrial relations; prospective changes to any of these;

— *communication and information flows*. Who communicates with whom; the means by which they communicate; why and when the communications takes place; communication networks; what information flows round the organisation; what access to internal databases and external public databases occurs; future trends in all of these;

— *the organisation's systems and procedures*. Current DP systems; formal company procedures; systems plans; computer terminals in use; user attitudes towards and experience of the introduction of advanced systems;

— *the external environment*. National and international Postal and Telecommunications regulations; British Telecom and Post Office plans for future services; data protection (privacy) legislation; standards; transborder dataflow regulations; future developments in all of these;

— *IMS products and services*. Currently available products and services; manufacturers plans; future availability of new products and services.

For further information, the reader is referred to Chapter 3, 'Collecting Information for the Strategy Study', in *Planning Office Automation— Electronic Message Systems* and to Chapter 4 'IMS: Types and Technology' of the present book.

4 IMS: Types and Technology

This chapter describes a classification of information and information management systems. It·then reviews some of the technology currently available for automating the management of information in offices. The vendors' products which are discussed have been chosen to illustrate features and facilities which either are typical for that type of system or because they illustrate some other point of interest. There are many other vendors (eg Prime, Wang, Xionics, Rediffusion, Aregon, GEC). Readers may receive up-to-date information about vendors and products for the electronic office from NCC's Enquiry Desk (see useful addresses, item 4.1).

INFORMATION CLASSIFICATION

There are four major classes of information:

— external information;

— operational information;

— administrative information;

— personal information.

These give rise to nine types of IMS (see Appendix C):

— public information databases;

— external *ad hoc* computing services;

— staff access to the corporate database;

— public access to the corporate database;

— internal *ad hoc* computing services;

— bulk storage of historical information;

— administrative information systems;

— update of administrative information;

— personal information systems.

Figure 4.1 illustrates these classes of information and categories of IMS. Other classifications are possible (eg based upon a division of information into external or internal, and a subdivision of internal information into personal or departmental or corporate). However, this classification should help organisations to perceive information as a resource and information management as an important issue in OA strategic planning.

External Information

It is now impossible for any manager or professional to read all the relevant journals or even those necessary to research for a book, report or lecture being prepared. Since the end of World War 2 there has been an information explosion of books, journals, reports, etc. Public libraries and abstracting services have helped greatly to save readers' time in identifying what they ought to read and in locating copies. However, much published information – it may be as high as 90% of the printed word – is redundant in the sense that it adds nothing new.

In the NCC office automation work programme, new (ie unpublished) information is gathered by NCC's professional staff through discussion with suppliers and users. Then books, reports, articles, conference papers, training material and other outputs are produced for dissemination to users. Although these outputs are directed at different audiences, there is inevitably some overlap and redundancy. Stibic (see Bibliography, item 4.1) has forecast that 'information overload' can be dealt with by significantly reducing the amount of redundancy in published information. This can be accomplished by means of:

— paperless publication (NB NCC is currently participating in the three-year BLEND electronic journal experimental project funded by the British Library Research and Development Department, administered by the Loughborough University of Technology Department of Human Sciences, and operated on a computer at the University of Birmingham);

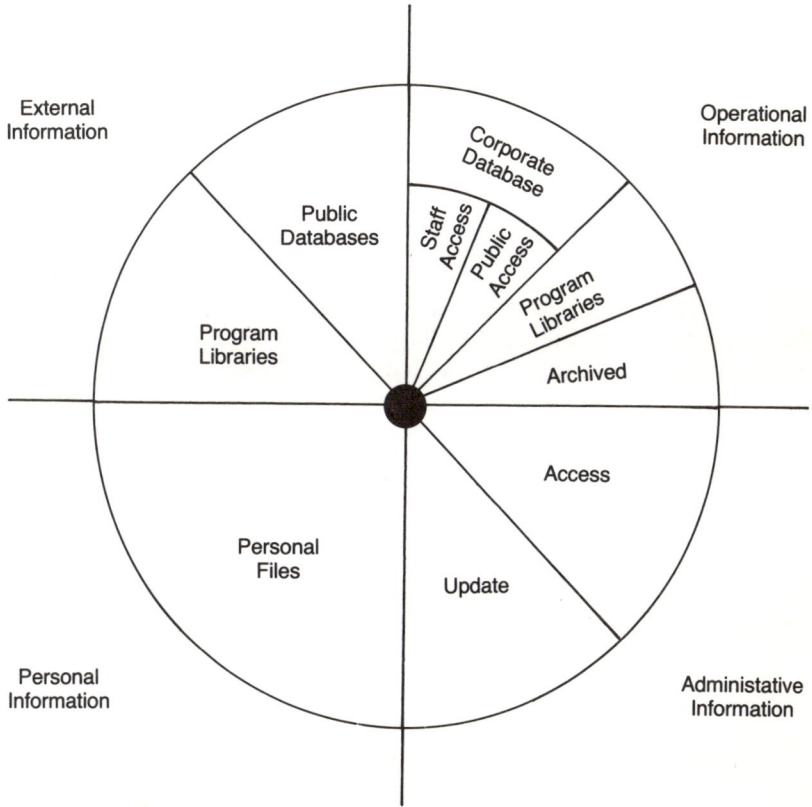

Figure 4.1   Types of Information and IMS

— on-demand publishing;

— structured publication;

— systematic storage and retrieval of elements of information.

Enquirers wishing to use a public database need to know what information is available and how to use it. They may be able to dial into the computer holding the database and go directly to the pages or frames of information of interest or be led there by menu-based searching or by browsing. Some services are not easy for inexperienced users to use, but trained staff will usually perform an on-line search.

Four types of public service can be highlighted:

— bibliographic information services;

— subscription databank services;

— British Telecom's Prestel viewdata service;

— bureau services.

Bibliographic information services include:

— the Dialog Information Retrieval Service provided by Lockheed Information Systems. Two large IBM computers are used, which can be accessed through the Tymnet and Telenet communications networks 22 hours a day. The Lockheed system has three ways in which database producers can offer information through the system – public files, sponsored files and private files. Public files are supplied to Lockheed who carry all charges and fix a price for users based on formatting costs and expected usage. Sponsored files remain completely under the control of the database supplier, who fixes the access price for users and pays all of Lockheed's costs. A sponsored file which is not publicly available, but is accessed only by organisations authorised by the database supplier, is called a private file, eg information which is very costly to gather and over which the database supplier wishes to exercise strict access control. The Dialog service contains over 45 million records providing references to magazine, journal and newspaper articles, conference papers, and technical reports in science, technology, social services, the humanities, business, economics and medicine, stored in more than 120 databases;

— the Systems Development Corporation (SDC) Search Service, which has more than 60 databases and which has been taken over by Burroughs Corporation;

— the European Space Agency Information Retrieval Service, which has more than 20 databases. This service is included in Euronet-DIANE and can be accessed through Euronet which is cheaper than IPSS. It receives funding from European governments to help close the gap between European usage of US databases (high) and US usage of European databases (low); (NB it has been estimated that in 1980 there were $2\frac{1}{2}$ million searches of US databases, over a third of which originated in Europe).

Subscription databank services include:

— ADP (the Association of Database Producers);

— Data Resources Inc.

Typically, a company gathers information, and provides a host computer and an access network, charging an annual subscription of £10,000 to users of the service.

British Telecom's Prestel has not grown as fast as forecast, neither in amount of information frames, nor in the amount of users or accesses. It was introduced in the autumn of 1978 on a trial basis and a public service was introduced just over a year later. By the end of 1980 60% of the population had local access. By February 1981 there were 180,000 frames of information and 8970 users, and this had grown by March 1982 to 210,000 frames and 14,000 users (11,800 business users and 2200 domestic users), with 150 Information Providers and 80 Sub-information Providers (who rent frames from the main Information Providers). It has been designed so that information which changes rapidly can be quickly and conveniently updated. The introduction of 'gateway' facilities was intended to increase Prestel traffic and the introduction of this facility in the London telephone area occurred in March 1982.

Bureau services include:

— SIA (this gives access to the ICI ASSASSIN package); SIA became a Euronet-DIANE host in 1981; together with the French CISI group it offers a wide range of econometric databanks; its files include:

  — IMF (International Monetary Fund) (financial time series);

  — OECD (main economic indicators);

  — PINCCA (price index numbers for current cost accounting in UK);

  — UKCSO (macroeconomic indicators);

  — UK Treasury macroeconomic forecasting model;

  — PPDS (physical property data service);

  — RHTM (regional highway traffic model).

Planned files include:

— a new Financial Times monitor databank, updated daily;

— CITIBANK USA economic indicators.

UK users can be switched directly through to CISI databanks, such as CRONOS-Eurostat, which is one of the largest European socio-economic databanks holding statistics in the form of time series on several different aspects of EEC economic activity including national accounts, general economic climate, fishing, agriculture, industry, external trade balance (import-export), energy, and macroeconomic indicators. USA users can access SIA via Telenet and Tymnet;

— Unilever Computer Services Limited (which has developed software called DECO containing facilities similar to those found in Lockheed's Dialog and Pergamon's Infoline); UCSL is also a Euronet-DIANE host and its services include an on-line public database (Fintel Company Newsbase) which includes data on 25,000 companies worldwide using company names, industry sectors, people, countries, products, business subjects discussed, organisation involved and date of publication;

— BOC Datasolve (this bureau, which provides a service for the STATUS package, was transferred from the BOC group to the Thorn-EMI electronic group under an agreement concluded early in 1982 and has become Datasolve – Thorn EMI).

The type of information management service now offered by such UK bureaux allows users to create and maintain databases which can then be made available for public access, or restricted to private in-house use.

In addition to the PSTN, there are a number of public networks to give access to information services such as those described above. In the USA there are the Tymnet network and the Telenet packet switched network. Since 1979 IPSS (the International Packet Switched Service) has provided a gateway from the UK into Tymnet and Telenet in the USA. Also in 1979, Euronet became operational and has been providing a commercial service since the beginning of 1980. It has replaced the European Space Agency's private network Esanet to give access from European countries to the Agency's computer centre at Frascati in Italy.

In 1981 British Telecom introduced its long-awaited public packet switched service PSS (now also referred to as SwitchStream 1). PSS will be vital to the development of the information industry outside the London telephone area since users would otherwise have to continue to pay long-distance line charges in addition to other costs and this constitutes a strong disincentive to searching databases from the regions. PSS will be linked to IPSS and to Euronet. Within five to ten years, satellite communications systems can be expected to become widely available. Their wideband transmission characteristics will allow large volumes of information to be moved about, and will support full text document retrieval, ie one-phase retrieval systems which will retrieve documents direct from the inquiry instead of two-phase retrieval systems which give on-line retrieval of abstracts from inquiries, followed by manual retrieval of documents from the abstracts.

Further information about on-line public information services may be found in the report *NCC Survey of On-Line Information Systems* (see Bibliography, item 4.2), in the publication *Directory of On-line Databases* (see Bibliography, item 4.3) which covers 600 databases available through 93 on-line service organisations and in the publication *On-line Bibliographic Databases* (see Bibliography, item 4.4) which gives details of nearly 200 databases containing 65 million references.

At some time in the future users can expect to be offered an alternative to conventional methods of obtaining the sort of information currently held in public databases and obtained by on-line searching and retrieval, as described above, or in books, manuals or directories.

The alternative method will involve optical disks which users will be able to purchase and mount as part of their in-house corporate database. Access will not involve British Telecom line charges nor the charges of the public service operator. Whether the one method or the other is preferable for a particular category of information will depend on:

— relative costs (cost of optical disk versus line charges and access charges/subscription charge);

— relative ease of access, search and retrieval;

— relative speed of obtaining information;

— how complete and up-to-date the information is.

A second type of IMS under the heading of external information is 'external *ad hoc* computing services'. This refers to access to external computers providing help in solving one-off or out-of-the-ordinary prob-

lems, such as financial modelling, statistical analysis or engineering calculations (as opposed to running standard company data processing applications packages). An example of this type of IMS is provided by the SIA
bureau service. It is possible for users to run powerful economic modelling, statistical and analytical programs against raw data on-line from a
desk-top workstation, using simple commands, representing time and
cost savings compared with alternative approaches for corporate business
analysts, researchers, administrators, etc.

It is interesting to note that in Japan push-button telephones can access
a central computer to perform complex mathematical computations.

Operational Information

There are four types of IMS which concern operational information:

— staff access to the corporate database;

— public access to the corporate database;

— internal *ad hoc* computing services;

— bulk storage of historical information.

The reader is referred to Appendix C for further information about
these IMS, but some additional comments will be made here.

Staff access to the corporate database is a rich area for bringing benefits
to employees. Enormous amounts of time are wasted at present by
employees trying to find out who holds information about various aspects
of the organisation's business, where it is, whether it is complete and
whether it is accurate. So formidable is the problem in non-automated
office environments that if attempts are made to discover such information they are often aborted. But if information is obtained it is committed
to paper or else it is forgotten; if it does get filed and if it can be retrieved
there is no knowing subsequently whether it remains accurate and complete or whether it has become out-of-date. In-house private viewdata
systems are dealing with this problem – giving immediate access to
information such as the following:

— manuals;

— directories;

— lists of products and their prices;

- in-house training courses and seminars;

- sports and social club notices;

- union notices;

- management notices;

- press releases;

- company and departmental budget and performance-to-date statistics.

(NB this information is distinct from records updated by, data input to and information output by DP systems, or the data processed by on-line transaction processing programs, which one has always been able to access from a computer terminal.)

An in-house private viewdata system can, therefore, not only give access to the corporate database of operational information, but also it can just as easily be used to give access to, disseminate and update administrative information. It can also access computers for computational and processing purposes. A new technology which is just beginning to emerge and will certainly develop further is the use of optical disks for storing and retrieving archived operational information, information from brochures, which comes into an organisation from outside, and other information which does not need to be frequently updated.

A proposal has been made to the CEC to link up European Community institutions, national ministries and parliaments with an integrated services information system. This system, INSIS (Interinstitutional integrated Services Information System), would employ digital network technology to combine voice and data on the same line – unlike dedicated data networks such as Euronet and the French Transpac, whose line bandwidths are not wide enough. Normal telephone lines cannot cater for facsimile transmission or data exchanges at the required speed. INSIS would combine – on the same lines – telephone, telex, teletex, terminal to computer transfers for word processing, facsimile or telecopying, teleconferencing, electronic mail and viewdata. This OA system would make decision-making faster, easier and of better quality, and improve the operation of the Community.

Administrative Information

Administrative information is text-based internal, corporate information which is not held in the corporate database as it is not used by data processing applications programs. There has been a progression in the last two to three years in the thinking behind how this type of information (see Appendix C) might be handled. With many organisations using word processors for document creation, for preparing text for books, reports etc, it was sensible to use word processors also to update files, lists, charts, manuals and other documents holding administrative information and to prepare an updated document which could then be printed or photo-copied and distributed through the internal mail. Nowadays organisa-tions are thinking in terms of giving office workers personal workstations with communications capabilities; and private viewdata systems – already used in some organisations, for access to, dissemination of, and the update of administrative information – seem to offer a very good way of automating the management of this type of information.

An alternative approach is not to use a viewdata approach but to use computer files. During a visit in December 1980 to the Research Centre of the Amoco Production Company in Tulsa, Oklahoma, one of the authors and a colleague found professionals with terminals linked by coaxial cables to a large IBM mainframe computer. Many preformatted frames are provided for the convenience of users entering administrative information, preparing standard memoranda, etc. One useful facility is that for scheduling conference rooms. Anyone can access and read the file containing this schedule, but only one person – the receptionist in this case – can write to this file. Users can book one of the seven conference rooms, if the display shows it to be available, by sending an electronic message through the system to the receptionist's mailbox. If the booking is urgent, the user can telephone the receptionist to confirm the booking.

Personal Information

The fourth category of information in the electronic office is personal information. Several office workers have in the last year or two been given a stand-alone personal microcomputer with applications programs stored on floppy disks to perform data processing applications in the financial area particularly, but also to aid budget control, planning and other tasks carried out by management and clerical workers. Others have had terminal access to a mainframe computer. In some organisations the microcomputer has been acquired as an attractive alternative to a main-frame for user departments who wish to pursue an independent line and to reduce their dependence upon the computer operations manager, who may not always give their work the same degree of priority as they have given it, and upon the computer systems development manager, who may not have sufficient resources to implement new applications as quickly as they would wish. Many organisations have tried to insist that user departments shall adhere to corporate guidelines in microcomputer selection so as to avoid problems in incompatibility, to have one set of standards, to minimise user training requirements and to take advantage of quantity discounts from suppliers.

An important new use for a personal computer is to allow a user to create, file, retrieve, edit, manipulate, share with colleagues, delete, etc personal information. In future multifunction workstations, personal computing and personal information management will be just two of the many functions which may be provided. Indeed for the majority of office workers, personal information management will be an essential feature of the multifunction workstation, while personal computing will not.

Personal information is distinct from personal computing, although personal information may include information which serves as input to, or is derived as output from, an applications program which executes either upon a mainframe computer or minicomputer to which the office worker's workstation has access or upon the workstation itself. There are many types of personal information, which office workers may wish to store in electronic form, such as:

— an index to documents held in the user's paper-based filing system; (NB ultimately individuals will cease to hold paper-based files, for paper documents will migrate to centralised filing systems maintained by ASCs, administrative support centres. Regrettably this migration will take longer to happen than it should. Documents held in paper-based filing systems, whether maintained by an individual or by an ASC, include books, reports, journals, cuttings, photocopies, slides and transparencies, etc);

— an index to the user's personal electronic filing system;

— draft text for inclusion in books, reports, articles under preparation;

— quotations from other people's speeches, books, reports, articles, newspapers;

— notes from meetings, telephone conversations, newspapers;

— calculations performed by computers;

— minutes and agendas;

— tickler file (ie a list of things to do);

— diary;

— filed electronic mail;

— planned use of time, progress reports and other information relating to work in progress;

— lists of names, addresses, telephone numbers, telex numbers and teletex numbers;

— diagrams, etc.

STORAGE MEDIA

The non-paper storage media which immediately come to mind for the storage of information are:

— magnetic disks (and drums);

— magnetic tapes;

— floppy diskettes;

— microfilm;

— microfiche.

Some disks are fixed and others are removable, including security copies whatever medium is used. Important issues in deciding what storage medium/media to use are:

— users should have a fast response time, so most of the information, except that which is infrequently accessed, should be stored on-line;

— managers and professionals do not want to have to handle floppy diskettes;

— storage space currently occupied by paper-based files should be released for more productive purposes.

The storage capacity of memory chips is increasing year-by-year and the shift which has already been in progress for several years – away from dumb terminals accessing mainframe computers with massive databases and towards dispersing computing power and storage capacity to departmental minicomputers and to individuals' workstations – will continue.

One major development, whose threshold has recently been reached and which OA strategy planners must take into account, is optical disk-based filing systems for documents, text, data and image information. The Matsushita microfile facsimile system illustrates another important development.

Another storage medium is bubble memory but there are indications that this technology has apparently not fulfilled its early promise.

TECHNOLOGY

Euronet-DIANE

An important external information service is Euronet-DIANE. DIANE stands for Direct Information Access Network for Europe. It is a major collaborative project by the member countries of the European Community. It brings together as partners:

— a number of major hosts in the European Community offering on-line scientific and technical information interactive retrieval services;

— the Community's PTTs (telecommunications authorities) who have built for this project a European international packet switched data transmission network called Euronet;

— the Commission of the European Communities as sponsors of the project and common services for the on-line user, such as:

— a common command language to allow users to search on different retrieval systems using one set of commands;

— European Community databases;

— enquiry and guidance service;

— improved document delivery systems;

— multilingual terminology databank;

— a users' forum;

— harmonisation of conditions of sale and billing and password procedures.

Euronet has packet switching exchanges in London, Paris, Frankfurt, Rome and Zurich, and access nodes in Dublin, Amsterdam, Brussels, Copenhagen and Luxembourg. A wide variety of terminals can access Euronet. Virtually all teletype-compatible terminals can be used for dial-up access, and a wider range of terminals can be connected by a leased line. Asynchronous transmission mode terminals, conforming to the ESP 20 protocol (or CCITT X28 recommendation) can be used on a dial-up basis at speeds of 110 to 300 bit/s and 1200/75 bit/s or with a lease line at speeds up to 1200 bit/s. Synchronous transmission mode terminals conforming to the CCITT X25 recommendation can be used with leased lines at speeds between 2400 bit/s and 9600 bit/s. Network tariffs are based on volume and time, not on distance, and are cheaper than making an ordinary international telephone call.

Following trials in 1978/79, preliminary traffic commenced on 15 November 1979 when Euronet was used free-of-charge by users accessing DIANE hosts. It was officially opened on 13 February 1980 and full commercial operation commenced on 31 March 1981. Subscribers to Euronet-DIANE have to obtain a Euronet telecommunications access password from their national PTT Euronet correspondent and conclude user contracts with the individual host services holding the relevant databases. The hosts issue their own passwords to control access to their databases.

After a year of commercial operation, there were 1500 Euronet-DIANE users, the number of hosts had increased from 12 to 25 – including British Library's BLAISE information service and Pergamon-Infoline in the UK, the European Patents Office, the German Institute for Medical Information (DIMDI), the German Information and Documentation Association (GID), the French Building Association (CATED), the German Energy, Physics and Mathematics Centre (INKA) and the European Space Agency's Information Retrieval Service (IRS) – and the number of on-line databases from 119 to 223. Subsequently two more UK hosts joined – SIA and Unilever Computer Services Limited. The 1981 Euronet-DIANE pocket directory, available free (see Useful Addresses, item 4.4), listed 291 available and planned databases and databanks and in April 1982 the DIANE on-line enquiry service listed 320, of which 80% were operational.

In December 1979, the Commission of the European Communities called for proposals for the development of new value-added information

services. 266 proposals were received by the CEC from European companies, universities and administrations for the development of services
which provide numerical or factual data using facilities such as information analysis, data manipulation or tailor-made information packages, or
for the extension of existing services from national to international level.
Twenty-six of these proposals were selected for funding and by March
1981 contracts had been placed with the thirteen organisations shown in
Figure 4.2.

To overcome the delay in receiving the printout from an on-line search,
when this is requested from the host computer, the European Space
Agency's Information Retrieval Service has located remote printers
nearer to users. These printers are attached by leased lines to the host
computer and handle several hundred thousands of lines per month. For
smaller quantities of printout, this leased line network approach is not
cost-effective and the CEC has developed a similar system which can be
operated over Euronet or other public packet-switched networks, based
upon a Remote Printing Protocol (RPP), which is a subset of the Network
Independent File Transfer Protocol (NIFTP) and which had previously
been implemented on the UK EPSS network. The RPP protocol allows a
remote printing station to be shared by several Euronet-DIANE hosts
and a particular host to print simultaneously on up to four different
remote printers. A printing station can work with two host computers at a
time and support a variety of printers and speeds from 120 characters per
second up to 600 lines per minute. Figure 4.3 illustrates the RPP concept.

An electronic mail service called Datamail was introduced on Euronet
by Datastar, a Euronet-DIANE host from Switzerland; for further
information, contact Datastar Marketing in Orpington, (see Useful
Addresses, item 4.5).

Towards the end of 1981 it was announced that it was possible in
certain circumstances for Prestel users in EEC countries, or Switzerland,
to use Euronet to access the Prestel computer instead of the normal
international telephone lines. This would save users some of their costs of
accessing Prestel. To use Euronet in this way, users require a Prestel-
compatible viewdata terminal with full keyboard – as well as a Euronet
access password from their national PTT Euronet correspondent.
Euronet users with teletype-compatible terminals cannot access Prestel,
because control signals sent from the Prestel computer would not be
understood.

	Organisation	Country	Project
1	Ergodata – Association d'Anthropologie Appliquee	France	Extension, in collaboration with the Universities of Kiel (Germany) and Birmingham (UK), of the data from the database on Ergonomy 'ERGODATA', in view of its use at Community level
2	Finsbury Computer Services Ltd	UK	The development of the TEXTLINE Service on companies, industries and products, economics, government and EC matters, etc
3	Learned Information (Europe) Ltd	UK	Multilingual and subject enhancement of 'Economic Abstracts International'
4	Centre D'Etudes Nucleaires de Saclay	France	System for information on grey literature in Europe (SIGLE)
5	Siamark International	Italy	Statistical database with analysis, modelling and forecasting facilities of world market raw materials indexes and prices
6	Groupement Scientifique Thermodata Europe (SGTE)	France	Databank of thermodynamic properties of inorganic and metallurgical mixtures including computational facilities
7	The Institute of Electrical Engineers (INSPEC)	UK	Electronic Materials Information Service
8	International Society for Ecological Modelling (ISEM)	Denmark	Databank on ecological parameters, environmental data and ecological models
9	The Pharmaceutical Society of Great Britain	UK	Martindale Drug Data Bank
10	Excerpta Medica	Netherlands	Databank of names of biologically-active substances
11	Anorganisch Chemisches Institut der Universitaet Bonn	West Germany	Databank on inorganic crystal structures
12	PIRA	UK	International Packaging Legislation Information Service (IPLIS)
13	Nederlands Maritiem Instituut	Netherlands	On-line maritime information service

Figure 4.2   CEC-Funded Developments for Value-Added Information Services

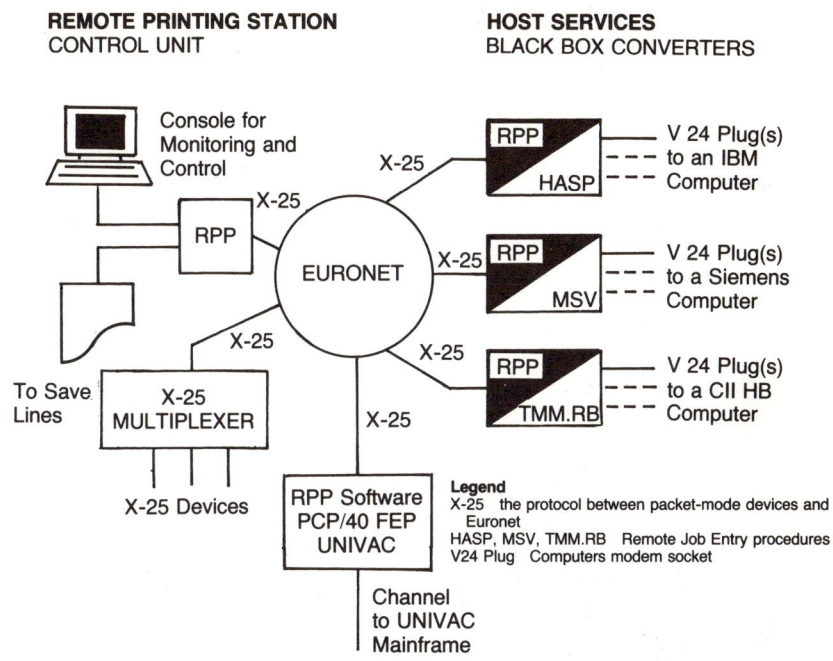

REMOTE PRINTING STATION
CONTROL UNIT

HOST SERVICES
BLACK BOX CONVERTERS

Console for Monitoring and Control

X-25

RPP
HASP — V 24 Plug(s) to an IBM Computer

X-25

RPP

EURONET

X-25 RPP
MSV — V 24 Plug(s) to a Siemens Computer

X-25

To Save Lines

X-25 MULTIPLEXER

X-25

X-25

RPP
TMM.RB — V 24 Plug(s) to a CII HB Computer

X-25 Devices

RPP Software PCP/40 FEP UNIVAC

Channel to UNIVAC Mainframe

Legend
X-25   the protocol between packet-mode devices and Euronet
HASP, MSV, TMM.RB   Remote Job Entry procedures
V24 Plug   Computers modem socket

Figure 4.3   Euronet-DIANE Remote Printing Concept

The CEC publishes a newsletter Euronet-DIANE News several times a year (see Useful Addresses, item 4.6).

It should be noted that CCITT are currently working to define recommendations for the use of teletex as a vehicle for information retrieval; recommendations may be adopted in 1984.

Viewdata

In the UK, the public viewdata system Prestel is operated by British Telecom. It is basically an on-line interactive information retrieval system using telephone lines as the transmission medium. There are public systems in other countries, notably Telidon (Canada), Teletel (France), Bildschirmtext (West Germany) and Captain (Japan). The facilities of Prestel have been enhanced since it was introduced as a public service early in 1980 and it is expected that they will continue to be, with the introduction of 'gateway' facilities during 1982 being a relevant development for OA strategy planning. There is a flourishing business in the UK in private viewdata systems with several in-house systems installed on computers and bureau services such as that of GEC Viewdata Systems Ltd and Interview, offered by Langton Information Systems and Mills & Allen, which is planned to be accessed through the Prestel Gateway service. Several important export orders have been won by UK companies such as Aregon International Ltd and Rediffusion Computers Ltd marketing viewdata software and technology. Contrast viewdata systems with teletext systems such as Ceefax and Oracle which provide information by broadcasting it, as TV programs are broadcast, but are not interactive.

Prestel employs alpha-mosaic graphics which means that its graphical figures are built up out of tiny lego-like elements. The graphical features of Telidon, which employs an alpha-geometric input system allowing the operator to construct graphical figures with a light pen, and of Captain (see below) have been favourably compared with those of Prestel; the preparation of graphical figures is easier and quicker and the resolution of the final product better.

In October 1981 Captain was still an experimental service used by 2000 terminals in the Tokyo Metropolitan Area. Some first hand information about it is mentioned here, because UK organisations must be made aware of what is happening elsewhere, and what information facilities competitors overseas may be using, and where appropriate demand that facilities available to them – whether on Prestel, or a private viewdata system, or any other information management system – are not inferior to those available to competitors. At the Captain Centre, at the Ginza Telephone Centre in central Tokyo, there are 16 input terminals creating between 1500 and 2000 frames of information daily. The system holds about 140,000 frames of information which will rise to 200,000 frames (NB similar to Prestel) in the current development. Many frames of information are updated regularly, eg news and weather information frames are updated daily, and a total of 440,000 different frames have been created since the system began its trials.

There are four types of information input terminal (IIT):

— tablet type (to input characters such as Kanji and Katakana and mosaic symbols by using a tablet, ie the user touches the character on the flat tablet);

— direct reading type (to input hand drawn figures and photographs using the principles used in facsimile systems; the contours or boundaries of figures can be recognised automatically, this makes colouring easy; it can also perform all of the functions of the tablet type IIT);

— keyboard type (to permit input characters such as Kanji and Katakana and mosaic symbols; Katakana characters input from the keyboard are converted into Katakana-Kanji mixed sentences);

— camera type (to permit input of characters, mosaic symbols, photographs and hand-drawn pictures, as in the direct character type of IIT. A TV camera is used to input figures and photographs. Enlargement, reduction and translation functions are provided for patterns).

Patterns (graphical figures) may be formed as mosaics, as in Prestel, using 180 kinds of pattern element. Patterns may also be formed by dot matrix giving a finer-grained display than mosaics. The ease with which the operator creates and edits hand-drawn patterns has to be seen to be appreciated.

Users are offered three information retrieval methods:

— via an index frame, menu-selection search (as in Prestel);

— via an eight-digit frame (page) reference number (like Prestel);

— via keywords (NB Prestel has an alphabetical index search for subjects);

and three services:

— ordinary retrieval service;

— closed user group service;

— order entry service.

The Japanese PTT Nippon Telegraph and Telephone Public Corporation (NTT) is assessing tariffs to introduce when commercial operation of its Captain system, scheduled for 1983, commences – at present, the terminal (the Captain monitor) and the information are free, the user pays only telephone line charges. The system is limited at present to those areas of the Tokyo telephone network with digital switching exchanges,

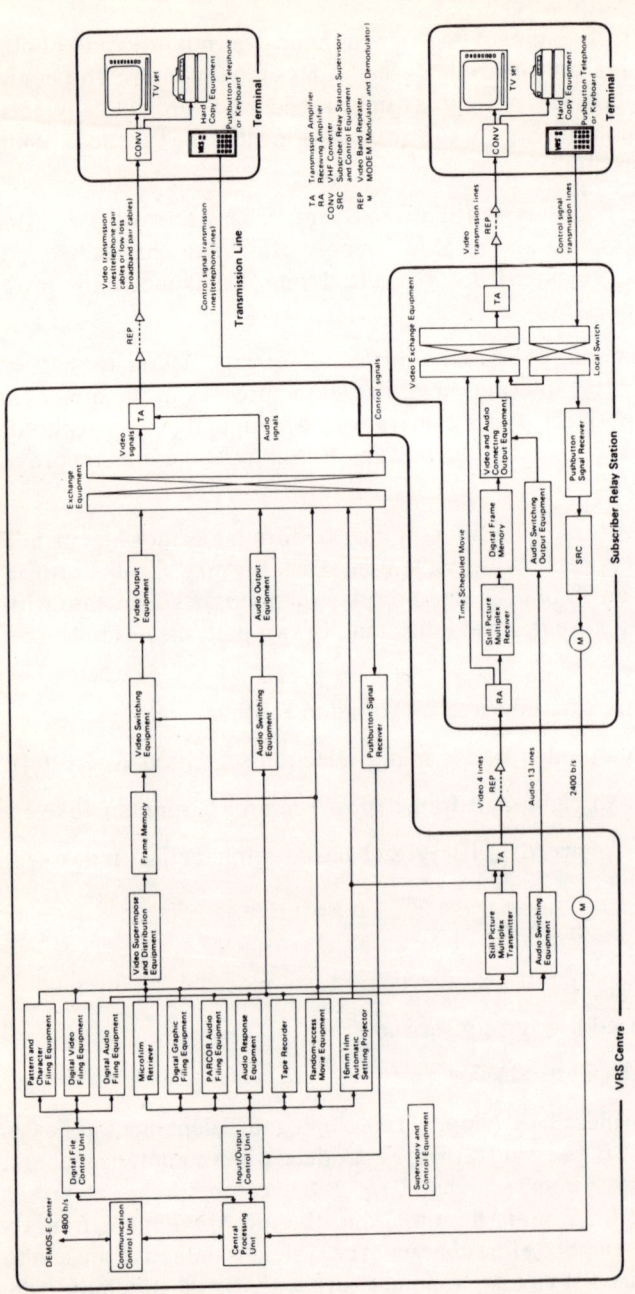

Figure 4.4 VRS (Video Response System) – System Configuration

rather than the traditional crossbar type. Many information providers wish to connect their mainframe host computer on-line to Captain, eg stock market firms, banks, travel organisations, hotels as well as computing bureaux. Five TV manufacturers and two computer manufacturers are involved in developing Captain for NTT, eg Nippon Electric Company (NEC) is developing the video plate camera-type IIT and Fujitsu is developing the keyboard-type text-input IIT.

An interesting, but as yet little known in the UK, Japanese information management system is NTT's experimental VRS (Video Response System). This is also an interactive visual information system. The VRS system configuration is illustrated in Figure 4.4.

VRS began operation in 1977 and has about 100 users in the Tokyo area. Surveys indicate that demand will grow faster in the business sector than in the domestic sector. Its response time is two seconds, compared with the ten seconds taken by Captain to scroll over a screenful of information. Three services are provided:

— still picture service (160,000 frames containing characters, graphics, photographs etc);

— time scheduled movie service (130 reels of video cassette tapes and 16-mm films);

— movies on request service (viewers' individual requests are selected and loaded by a computer-controlled electro-mechanical system) prior to transmission.

Mixed displays of still pictures and motion pictures are possible. The video transmission lines employ a baseband transmission system of an individual wiring type using balanced twin cables (telephone pair cables or low loss broadband pair cables). An audio-video simultaneous transmission system is employed to share pilot signals and audio carriers and to transmit audio signals by overlapping them on video signals. There are repeater stations every 500 metres. VRS applications are illustrated in Figure 4.5, and Figure 4.6 illustrates the video and audio equipment characteristics. Studies are being made into optical fibre and laser beam information transmission, and new high-definition image processing, which may lead to the integration of VRS with Captain, and to video conferencing.

Features, not available on current Prestel sets, will include:

Information retrieval and information services:

— information on various commodities in sales activities

— marketing

— inventory control

— manufacturing processes

— parts control

— medical information service (remote diagnosis, etc)

— domestic information service (shopping, leisure, and other information)

— pictures of property for sale

— promotional films

Computer-aided instruction:

— employee training in companies

— audio-visual education and training in educational organisations

— acquisition of qualifications at home

— adult education

— linguistic education

Entertainment:

— quizzes

— games

Figure 4.5   VRS (Video Response System) – Applications

— 16 colours;

— full screen background colour;

— black foreground colour;

— double width characters;

— underlining.

Category	Equipment	Information	Capacity	Average Access Time	Notes
Still Picture	Digital video filing equipment	Colour still picture	4,000 frames /400 MB disk pack	0.2 sec.	–
	Pattern and character filing equipment	Character, graphic (monochrome, colour)	100,000 to 150,000 frames /200 MB disk pack	0.1 sec.	Characters:5,000 Colours: 60
	Digital graphic filing equipment	Colour graphic	4,000 frames /100 MB disk pack	0.1 sec.	Colours: 60
Movie	16mm film automatic setting projector	Movie	10 reels Max. 70 min./reel	–	For time scheduled movie service
	Random-access movie equipment	Movie	120 video cassette tapes 12 VTRs	11 sec.	For composite picture service request movie service
Audio	Digital audio filing equipment	Explanatory comment on each picture	4,000 messages /200 MB disk pack (10 sec./message)	0.2 sec.	–
	PARCOR audio filing equipment	Explanatory comment on each picture	8,000 messages /100 MB disk pack (10 sec./message)	0.1 sec.	–
	Audio response equipment	System message etc.	512 words /4 MB drum (1.1 sec./word)	0.5 sec.	–
	Tape recorder	Music	Max. 7 min (endless tape)	–	For background music

Figure 4.6 VRS (Video Response System) – Video and Audio Equipment

This is, of course, only the beginning, for manufacturers have to adopt the standard, and there is the question of accessing other systems such as Telidon and Captain. Also it is interesting to think simultaneously of NTT's VRS system and UK optical fibre transmission developments, communications satellite developments and cable TV proposals and the opportunities for:

— new jobs;

— the emergence of an information society (in business and domestically);

— the potential to export new technology and systems;

— Japan's Fifth Generation Computer Systems Project.

In some instances, users have a choice between two alternative approaches – viewdata systems and external databases – when seeking to retrieve information. There are many more terminals which can access databases than there are viewdata terminals that can access Prestel (14,000 terminals), Bildschirmtext (5000 terminals), Teletel (3000 terminals), Captain (2000 terminals) or other systems, although the use of public viewdata is slowly growing and the cost of a TV set adapted to receive viewdata is low compared with that of a computer terminal (which is itself low compared with the cost of a multifunction workstation). (NB Ultimately in the fully-integrated electronic office each person will have a multifunction workstation appropriate to specific needs and viewdata will be one of its functions.)

Users also have a choice between storing certain information internally in viewdata format, using an in-house private viewdata system, or in a computer database format, using an information retrieval package such as IBM STAIRS. The user must decide which method is more appropriate for different types of information and different users' needs. It is interesting to note that Langton Information Systems have a software package called Preview which automates the process of building and maintaining viewdata format databases. It converts information from conventional computer databases into viewdata format and structure.

In the UK, British Telecom is developing Picture Prestel (see Bibliography, item 4.5), a facility similar to the still picture facility of NTT's VRS. Just as newspapers, magazines and books contain photographs, it is natural to suppose that the move towards electronic publishing must lead to the transmission of still pictures of the quality of broadcast television. Some private viewdata systems in the UK already have still picture facilities.

The development of viewdata standards is an important matter, for at present there are different specifications for terminals for Prestel, Teletel, Bildschirmtext, etc. Two different methods of generating graphics are employed:

— alpha-mosaic method, using a mosaic of dots;

— alpha-geometric method, using geometric elements (eg circles, arcs, diagonal lines).

The 26 member countries of CEPT (European Conference on Posts and Telecommunications) have completed three years of work and agreed in 1981 on a standard for the next generation of viewdata terminals. Terminals built to this standard will be able to receive information from these three European public viewdata systems.

Prestel was introduced as an information distribution system, and has been enhanced with closed user group and message facilities. Despite this, usage remains disappointingly low, although rising. The introduction of 'Gateway' facilities in 1982 (software purchased by British Telecom from the West German PTT who had commissioned it for their Bildschirmtext viewdata service) has been seen as giving Prestel a 'shot in the arm'. 'Gateway' refers to software which will provide a link between privately-run computers and databases and Prestel. Initially twelve information providers' computers will be able to be accessed via the Prestel gateway. Subsequently there are expected to be 'umbrella' gateways giving links from a privately-run computer (which a user has accessed via the Prestel gateway) to yet another computer or computers.

This will tend to open up both in the UK and Western Europe the public and private database markets, as compared with now – not to mention Euronet-DIANE enhancements which are developing in parallel and which will have a similar impact. Soon, then, Prestel gateway facilities will enable an information provider to offer users three levels of service:

— access to the database held on the information provider's mainframe;

— as above, plus access to the mainframe for computational and processing services;

— access, routed through the information provider's mainframe, to databases on other computers.

Prestel's gateway will allow direct communication between a user and an information provider's computer without the information having to be loaded on the Prestel computer. It will also allow an information provider who did not want to administer a charging system to use Prestel to monitor usage charges.

Two impressive private viewdata systems seen during 1981 are mentioned below. One was developed following a trial of Prestel in 1978/1979 and runs on the Texas Instruments DS 990 series of minicomputers under the DX10 operating system. The evaluation of this trial indicated that a viewdata system could be justified because it would give a faster flow of information to salesmen and this would lead to an increase in sales and a reduction in the cost of securing orders. The private viewdata system was developed because there were no plans at that time by the Post Office (now British Telecom) for Prestel to be enhanced during the following two or three years in a way which would meet the requirements of the company. So successful has the system been that its use has been extended beyond the sales force during 1981 into such areas as:

— the receptionist's desk;

— the personnel department;

— the main open-plan office;

— the research and development office;

— the computer room;

— presentation rooms (NB it is interesting to note that viewdata is a very good medium for giving presentations; information frames in colour holding text, data, graphs and diagrams replace overhead foils; presenters can quickly and easily prepare their own visuals, calling upon a library of graphical features stored within the system, and do not have to carry paper, flip charts, foils or anything else to the presentation room);

— factories.

It is important to note three points about this IMS:

— it was not justified by cost savings, but by the added value benefits it was expected to bring (and did bring); if the company had imposed a constraint that the system must bring cost savings it would not have been implemented and consequently the company would probably have lost its competitive edge and turnover would have dropped;

— once it was installed and being used for the sales force, its extension into offices was not difficult to justify; this is an example of 'piggy-backing' where once system development costs have been justified for the first application, only the marginal costs of additional viewdata terminals and software enhancements have to be justified;

— technological developments such as voice recognition systems, electronic funds transfer, electronic mail and point-of-sale terminals could dramatically impact the modus operandi of travelling salesmen in the medium term, if not in the short term; conceivably the viewdata system could become of major importance in the offices and of lesser importance for the sales force for whom it was originally developed.

Similarly, the second private viewdata system is having an impressive impact on office work at the organisation's head office in Swindon, Wiltshire. The company has embarked upon a ten-year programme to get rid of paper in offices. The company has a WAR ON PAPER policy statement which mentions that it was making 53 million photocopies a year, about 230,000 per working day, and that this is harmful to the company's well-being. The avoidance of paper will bring savings in:

— envelopes;

— postage;

— paper;

— reading time;

— filing time;

— photocopying time.

In the War on Paper section of this company's viewdata system there is a frame containing a directive from the company chairman that a high proportion of paperwork will no longer be issued; its discontinuance will force office workers to use the system to obtain information. One of the most impressive features of the system, or more accurately perhaps of the application of the system within the company, is the enormous amount of up-to-date corporate information about the company's plans and performance which can be accessed by anyone authorised to do so.

There were, in December 1981, about 80 viewdata terminals in the company's head office, where overall administration and financial administration for the company and its subsidiary companies is carried out, and another 150 terminals at other locations for subsidiary companies to use for their own internal operational and administrative needs. There are short-term plans to build a private communications network to allow the system to be extended to another 1900 users (1139 UK showrooms, 173 non-UK showrooms and 600 support offices). In the longer term, the system could be used by other companies who have business with the company such as the window cleaning contractors, to make enquiries about the payment of invoices and so on.

The company's philosophy for gaining commitment to the system from employees is simple and straightforward, but regrettably not often found in UK organisations. It is worth repeating here:

— go in at the top from the Chairman downwards; let managers lead their subordinates by the example they set;

— withdraw paper-based information distribution;

— provide frames of interesting information (eg job vacancies, sports and social club events, quiz competitions in which users fill in answers on frames and can win worthwhile gifts as prizes);

— provide terminals in corridors, etc wherever people actually congregate and spend their time (in addition to providing them in offices where people need them to do their work);

— insist on standards for indexes, but allow users to create the actual information frames in any format they wish.

Benefits include:

— progress along the migration path to the paperless office;

— saved time, which can be used to add value;

— everybody accesses and uses the same information which is up-to-date and consistent;

— managers do not attend meetings with paper; meetings are held in offices with a viewdata terminal and the terminal is used throughout the discussions at meetings;

— through integration, there are four modes of creating frames:

  — manually from the keyboard;

  — via a word processor;

  — via output from a computer process;

  — from accessing the database on the mainframe computer.

Viewdata systems can therefore be used for many purposes. Detailed information to assist organisations, who have decided to use public and/or private viewdata systems, to evaluate the systems which are currently available and to make a selection is contained in NCC's *Viewdata Systems – A Practical Evaluation Guide* (see Bibliography, item 1.7). This book is one of a series giving guidelines for the evaluation and selection of OA products. It describes the criteria which should be considered in the evaluation, viz:

— functional criteria:

  — system specification (system security features, editing facilities, mailbox facilities, response frames, data processing interface, accounting statistics);

  — the user terminal (colour or monochrome, size, capabilities, controls, display features, modem, auto-dialling, memory, direct page memory store, connection sockets, control keypad);

  — the editing keyboard;

— ease of use criteria:

  — Prestel standards;

  — information format;

  — system language;

  — routeing and indexing;

  — ergonomics (screens, keyboards);

— user support (user documentation, technical enquiry service);

— supplier criteria:

— vendor characteristics;

— product package (delivery date, installation, user training,
   documentation, warranty period, maintenance);

— product reputation.

Document Filing

Organisations must plan how to reduce the space occupied by paper files
and the manpower used in maintaining, searching through and retrieving
information from paper-based filing systems. As the storage capacities of
non-paper storage devices rise, and their costs fall, documents may be
stored electronically, or abstracts (or keywords) only may be stored.
However developments will occur in the next year or two which will have
an impact on thinking about document filing and it is unwise to be
dogmatic at this time.

One point of view is that users would want to store complete documents electronically. The document has to be prepared initially in some
way – by creating text at a word processor, for example. Once it exists,
users would not want to spend any more time than is absolutely necessary
in annotating it, or in preparing keywords or abstracts. The complete
document should be scanned and filed. It can then be retrieved whenever
the user refers to any string of characters contained in it. Furthermore a
copy of the document can be edited to produce new documents. Products
to support this point of view can be expected to be developed in Japan and
elsewhere.

Another point of view is that documents should not be stored electronically unless they are generated that way. So a letter, an administrative
memorandum, a personal tickler file, a frame of information about the
prices of an organisation's products prepared for a private viewdata
system etc would be keyed in at a workstation and the complete document would remain available in electronic form for as long as required.
But other documents, particularly those which come into the organisation
in paper form from outside (eg letters, reports, brochures, photographs,
journals, etc), but also some internally generated documents (perhaps

foils for presentations, photographs, drawings, untyped handwritten documents, etc) would not be stored electronically as complete documents – only reference information about each.

In the past, organisations would have opted for the second approach for technological and cost reasons, but in the future many things which used to be impossible or impractical will become feasible. One organisation which has operated a very successful document filing system of this latter type for four years is the Amoco Research Centre at Tulsa, which introduced the EOS (Electronic Office System) software late in 1977.

Electronic filing is so successful that, at the time of a visit in December 1980, no filing cabinets had been bought since EOS was introduced in the offices of professionals and managers. There is a centralised filing system in the office of the administrative secretary and documents (eg incoming letters, magazine clippings) are given a serial number by the computer and stored in chronological order.

An administrative secretary creates an entry in the electronic filing system by specifying and keying in a subject heading; also keyed in is information about from whom, to whom and date of the document to be filed. The secretary chooses the subject title of about 120 characters although managers/professionals can specify this if they wish to, eg to assist them to retrieve it, by ringing words in the text and passing the document to the administrative secretary. When a letter arrives an administrative secretary (when authorised to do so by the recipient) indexes it and keys this indexing information into the computer. The computer issues a number which determines its position in the chronologically organised central filing system and the administrative secretary physically files it in that position. Anyone interrogating EOS may learn of the existence of the letter or whatever and, if interested in reading it, can retrieve it from the filing system using the computer-generated serial number.

All searching of the electronic filing system is performed from a screen terminal by professionals and managers themselves using subject, date, author, keywords, etc. They do not have to try to remember where they filed a document; they do not have to ask a colleague to remember where it was filed; they do not have to ask a secretary to remember what happened to it. Once a document is electronically filed, it is current policy that it should not be destroyed, although a person who has been given the means to retrieve it can erase the ability to retrieve it; by this type of housekeeping activity the index file can be reduced in size and search times reduced.

OCR and Facsimile

In Japan especially, the technologies of optical character recognition (OCR) and facsimile have advanced a long way and will continue to do so, because of the complexity of the Japanese written language and the difficulty of entering text through a keyboard as compared with the English language with its 26 character alphabet. (For this reason, voice input and recognition technologies will also advance quickly.)

In the UK, just as anywhere else in the world, a very important issue bearing upon the usefulness of electronic IMS is how easily, cheaply and quickly information can be converted into digital form in the first instance. Existing products and technological developments in Japan suggest that UK user organisations must look very carefully into the role which OCR products and integrated OCR/facsimile products can play.

In Japan, letters and postcards have three preprinted red rectangular boxes into which numerical, not alphanumerical, information is hand-written. This information allows 'automatic handwritten postal code numerical reader-sorter' machines to achieve a reliable, high-speed performance. A reader-sorter developed by Toshiba was installed in the Tokyo Central Post Office in 1966 and a year later the Japanese Ministry of Postal Services introduced the Japanese Postal Code Number System; by 1981, 200 large post offices had been automated. About 80% of addresses are handwritten and nearly 95% of regular size mail items can be recognised with an error rate of less than 1%. The speed attained is 25,000 pieces of mail per hour (ie seven per second).

Another pattern recognition machine, developed by Toshiba, reads books and other typed/printed documents with Kanji ideogram characters at a speed of 100 Kanji characters per second, and an accuracy of 99.8% from a stored memory of 2000 Kanji characters. What levels of performance might be achieved in the future employing more sophisticated chip technology, with a stored memory not of 2000 Kanji characters, but just the numerals, upper- and lower-case letters of the English language alphabet, punctuation marks and some special characters?

An impressive OCR machine at Tokyo's Data Show 81 exhibition was the Xondex 8000. This machine is claimed to have a reading accuracy of 99.99% and a speed of 100 handwritten characters a second. Unreadable characters can be easily corrected through the machine's keyboard and screen. The machine stands on a floorspace of 5 square metres. It can read 26 upper-case letters of the alphabet, 10 numerals and 30 special characters. Scanned information can be displayed, printed, stored on floppy diskette, punched or transmitted.

At the Matsushita OA Centre in the Chuo-ku district of Tokyo we saw the ODEFAS (On-line Data Entry Facsimile System) – a facsimile machine with information processing capability, a combined OCR/facsimile machine and a microfile facsimile system.

At Toshiba's Research Laboratories at Kawasaki near Hanida Airport, we saw an integrated facsimile/OCR system under development. Documents of standard format can be sent via facsimile to the central facsimile/OCR machine, where the received document is scanned by OCR and the information passed on to the computer for processing. The OCR scanner reads only the clearly defined alphanumeric characters handwritten on certain parts of the document; any other annotations or format designs being effectively ignored. The implications are that handwritten (ie 'printed' rather than naturally written) information can be easily input from a remote site (eg an office) to a central processor. Natural handwriting is unlikely to be recognised for a few years yet, perhaps by about 1991, but the implications of this technology for storing incoming typed and printed documents and brochures are clearly important.

It should be noted that CCITT is discussing Group IV facsimile recommendations concerned with the mixing of character coded text and digitised image. Mixed mode (text and image, initially) is also under discussion in the context of teletex, but does not of course include OCR capability.

Content Addressable File Storage

An important addition to the conventional processing of COBOL serial files or structured databases such as ICL's IDMS is the ability to also access information using Content Addressable File Stores (CAFS) (see Bibliography, items 4.6 and 4.7).

CAFS is a hardware solution to the problem of retrieving data from sequential, relational and structured databases, as well as from loosely structured text such as legal documents and technical papers. CAFS enables data to be retrieved for processing at the speed at which it comes off the disk on which it is stored.

While a record is being searched for fields which match the selection criteria submitted by the user, a parallel mechanism extracts from the record those fields of data which the user has requested and passes them to the mainframe computer. The parallel electronics is claimed to be essential for free text searching of data which is not rigidly formatted.

The CAFS controller relieves the host computer of the task of retrieving records from disk, reading them to see if they are relevant and discarding them if they are not. It retrieves and passes to the mainframe only those records which are relevant, giving high throughput to batch processing programs, fast response to enquiries and cheaper file access by eliminating redundant processing inside the mainframe. How does it do this? Suppose an enquiry 'GET NAME, PERSONNEL NO. FOR JOB EQUAL ARCHITECT AND SCALE AC1 AND LANGUAGES EQUAL SWEDISH OR GERMAN' is submitted. Then the functional subsystems of the CAFS controller will:

— test the search arguments (eg JOB EQUAL ARCHITECT) (in its Key Channel Unit);

— test whether or not all search arguments are satisfied (in its Search Evaluation Processor);

— retrieve RELEVANT records (in the Record Retrieval Unit).

A feature of CAFS is that it does not insist on precise search arguments, but can accept 'fuzzy' data; for example if one had heard a man's name but was uncertain whether it was spelt REID, READ, or REED, one could enter RE?D in the enquiry statement.

ICL has announced two products which use CAFS techniques.

A new product was launched in April 1982 to widen the attractiveness of CAFS. CAFS Information Search Processor (CAFS-ISP) is an integrated product in both hardware and software terms on the 2966 range of processors using the VME 2900 operating environment. The hardware option is priced at approximately £50,000 and attaches to the standard disk controller used for the ICL Modular Disk Storage System devices. This hardware option can be attached to each disk channel, giving a present maximum disk storage of 80 Gigabytes able to be searched by CAFS-ISP. The standard Data Management Software products are used to exploit the CAFS-ISP hardware and standard files and databases are used unchanged. Using the powerful ICL range of Application Development Tools a user can write specific applications to take advantage of CAFS techniques and facilities.

CAFS 800 continues to be sold as a subsystem for about £170,000 and as part of a CAFS Information System including processor from about £280,000.

At the time of announcing CAFS-ISP, which will be available in 1983, ICL also announced a strategy to include CAFS products for connection to its Distributed Resources Systems. In particular the CAFS Information Server (CAFS-IS) will operate in office systems to handle data and text in a coherent manner with plans to add voice later. CAFS-IS will significantly make CAFS available to users through the local area network as part of the ICL Network Product Systems.

Benefitting from the 1981 agreement with Fujitsu, ICL will be able to take advantage of this Japanese company's advanced chip technology and the price of CAFS will fall from around £175,000 to around £50,000 for CAFS-ISP and much lower for CAFS-IS. In the UK, CAFS is also available through the Computel Ltd computer service bureau (see Useful Addresses, item 4.7).

A USA CAFS development is the Britton-Lee Intelligent Database Machine (IDM). When it was launched in the UK in September 1981 as a cheaper (from $80,000) alternative to the ICL CAFS product, there were alreadly 32 customers in the USA. IDM is a hardware-matching device based on the relational database design of the University of California, at Berkeley. Data is held in tables on disk and is retrieved by matching against a query using special purpose hardware. The user could use a microcomputer or office workstation to convert the commands of whichever inquiry language is used into machine language commands, with the IDM often used as a back-end processor to a mainframe. The IDM is designed with a very high speed bus in the controller, which achieves high speed instead of paralleling hardware on the disks (see Bibliography, item 4.8).

Several people have told us that a CAFS-type full-text search capability was essential, or at least desirable. However one experienced user of an electronic filing system, which requires users to specify keywords for document searching and retrieval in the header, felt (in 1980) that it was not necessary and was too expensive.

Xerox 8000 Network System

An electronic office system available from Xerox is the Xerox 8000 Network System (NS). This uses a local area network based on the concept of distributed information processing, which allows for common service sharing. Its foundation is the Ethernet network.

A variety of devices such as workstations (up to a maximum of 1024) can be attached to a single shielded coaxial cable. Baseband signalling is employed and data is transmitted at a rate of 10 million bit/s. The workstations have access to shared services on the network and presently allow users the following facilities:

— electronic filing;

— electronic mail;

— electronic printing;

— communications gateways and multiplexers to remote devices and networks (such as terminals, host mainframes and external public services).

Equipment which can be attached directly to Ethernet includes:

— Xerox 860 Information Processing System (for text processing, records processing, etc);

— Xerox 8010 Professional Workstation (see below);

— Xerox 8000 NS File Server (see below);

— Xerox 8000 NS Print Server (see below);

— Xerox 8000 NS Communications Server (see below);

— Xerox 8000 NS Communications Interface Units.

The 8010 workstation has been designed to meet the needs of professionals, middle management and specialist staff whose prime job is to acquire information from many sources and to review, edit, extend and present it to others for assessment or action. Amongst other facilities, it has formatting facilities to allow users to experiment with different presentation formats and page layouts, and graphics facilities to allow the precise positioning of text or graphics; and to help with the generation of squares, rectangles, triangles, circles, ovals and various arrowhead styles, lines of varying thickness and style (solid, dotted, dashed, dot-dashed, double, vertical, horizontal, diagonal, straight, curved), tables and forms. It has facilities to help a professional to create and maintain lists, directories, records and reports, and to sort, filter and reformat records. The user can access data from a host computer, extract, analyse and organise it, and combine it with additional text or graphics to produce a new report. Its facilities can be enhanced by software options for:

— complex mathematical equations;

— automatic checking for spelling errors;

— advanced graphics (bar charts, pie charts and curve graphs);

— communications with non-Xerox workstations and host computers not on the Ethernet network.

It is one of a range of user workstations which co-operate to satisfy a variety of applications. For example, the Xerox 860 Information Processing System is a powerful, stand-alone text processing product which can be enhanced and attached to the local area network. Thereupon bulk text documents originated on it can be filed, mailed and exchanged with an 8010, which allows the user comprehensive enhancement tools.

It has been noted that the 8010 does not yet have voice processing facilities integrated into its operation and it remains to be seen to what extent (if at all) this omission proves to be a drawback to users of its other excellent features.

The File Server provides electronic filing and file management facilities for users to improve the efficiency of storage and retrieval functions and to reduce the need for hard-copy printout of information. There are (in electronic form) file drawers (containing folders, documents and record files), which may be opened and closed by authorised users. File management facilities include open, close, list, create, store, retrieve, move and copy functions. The file management system replicates familiar manual processes.

The Print Server is a shared resource available both to workstations directly connected to the local area network and to others in remote sites which make up a totally distributed system through the software provided. The Print Server controls a high resolution (300 x 300 spots/inch) electronic printer subsystem using laser-xerography technology and producing output on cut-sheet, plain A4 paper at 12 pages per minute. It handles portrait or landscape output formats for a wide range of type fonts and styles. In conjunction with the 8010 workstation it prints graphic illustrations and forms with equal facility, mixed with text, and in many applications takes the output needs in one step to 'camera-ready' copy.

A local network allows its users to benefit from new technology to automate the document preparation tasks at the office worker's desk, the sending and receiving of text messages which flow between users attached to the local network, and the management of personal information and information which can be shared with other network users – and all of these activities together account for a large part of what office workers do. However no system is complete unless it has links to other networks, to other sites, to external public databases, to the corporate mainframe computer (for access to the corporate database and to the computational power of the mainframe), to British Telecom services, etc. The Communications Server provides a full-duplex facility connecting with local/remote workstations, terminals and host computers. Data transmission mode may be asynchronous, byte or bit synchronous at rates up to 9600 bit/s. Its 'gateway' service allows stand-alone devices at the local site or at a remote location to be interfaced with the Communications Server, so that remote workstations in offices which cannot justify a local Ethernet can nevertheless participate in the Xerox 8000 network applications. The 'internetwork routeing' service allows separate Ethernets to be interconnected for the purpose of sharing resources and information.

Another Xerox workstation is the Xerox 820. This is a desk-top microcomputer with a range of business-oriented applications software packages operating under the CP/M operating system. Further information about Xerox products in the UK can be obtained from Rank Xerox (UK) Ltd, who installed an operational Ethernet at their London office early in 1982.

Burroughs OFIS1 Office Information System

Another electronic office system is the OFIS1 Office Information System offered by Burroughs, announced in June 1981 and demonstrated at Info 82 in London in February 1982. A typical OFIS1 configuration for

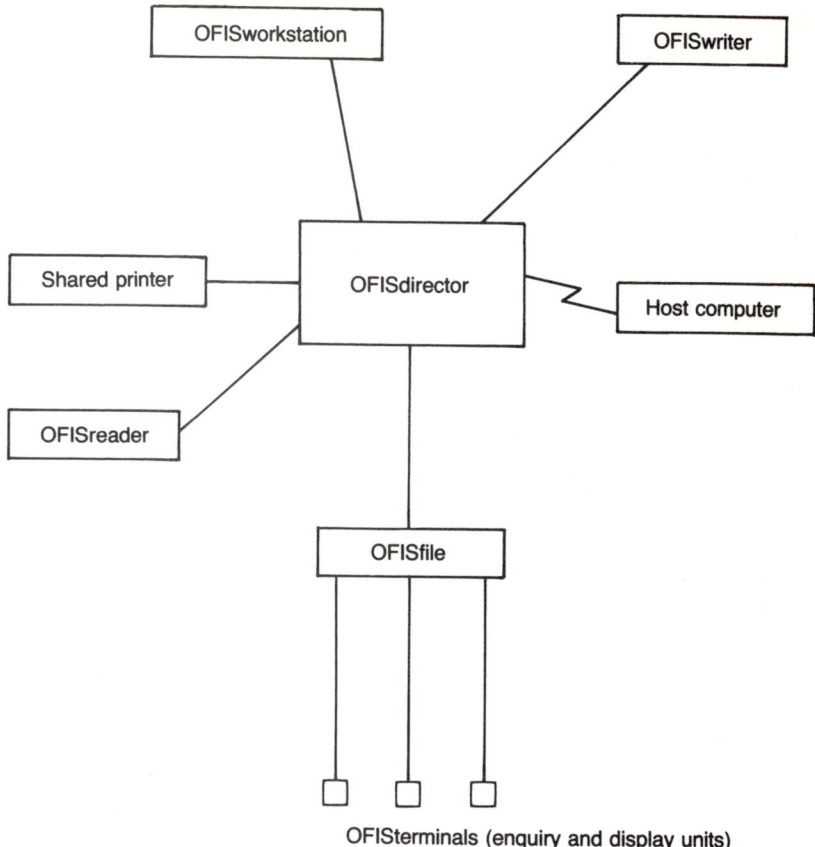

Figure 4.7   An Office Information System Configuration – Burroughs OFIS1

document creation and revision, information storage and retrieval by content, and resource sharing is shown in Figure 4.7.

A key element in OFIS1 is the OFISfile electronic filing system which holds 160 Mbytes of information on fixed disk inside a unit whose dimensions are 22in wide by 34½in long by 31in high. It stores electronically the equivalent of about 80,000 A4 pages. Documents, letters etc held in OFISfile are retrieved by content so there is no need to annotate them with keywords or abstracts (summaries) when they are stored. A search may be made for all documents containing, say, the phrase 'office automation' (and synonyms also, if desired) and the user receives a menu of all documents meeting this criterion, from which documents can be selected for display. To assist the user to find the documents which he is looking for or to locate any which are relevant to an inquiry, the search process will look for words which are mis-spelled, which are in a different order or which take alternative forms such as plurals, possessive or participles. Documents which are to be stored in OFISfile may be generated by a word processor or terminal linked to OFISfile or OFISdirector (see below), but they may also be entered via OFISreader which is a high-speed OCR page reader that accepts text typed on conventional electric typewriters or other manufacturers' word processors.

Another key element of OFIS1 is OFISdirector – the communications management component of the system which is the link that enables other elements of the system to intercommunicate and to share resources (ie working files, printers, OFISreader and OFISfile). It is also the gateway that links an OFIS1 system to OFIS1 systems in other departments of an organisation as well as to the information held on computers and to the computation power of computers – computers within the organisation, computers holding public databases and computers at service bureaux. OFISdirector also provides personal productivity tools such as:

— electronic mail;

— calender;

— conference scheduler;

— distribution lists;

— tickler file;

— personal files.

Other OFIS1 components include:

— the OFISwriter word processor;

— the OFISterminal enquiry and display unit for senior managers and executives; (NB this unit does not allow the user to input information into an OFISfile nor to alter information already stored there);

— the OFISworkstation keyboard and display unit; (NB this unit can input to an OFISfile and can access and amend information already stored there; it can access other OFIS1 components and other systems via OFISdirector);

— OFISfax facsimile equipment allowing externally-generated correspondence and documentation to be digitised, stored, communicated and reproduced in original form.

It is anticipated that yet-to-be-announced OFIS products will integrate voice and video transmission and will utilise optical fibre and satellite communications.

ICL PERQ Professional Workstation

In 1981 ICL launched an up-market scientific and graphics computer called the PERQ aimed at office professionals, rather than the mass market. This consists of:

— a free-standing desk-top display unit (approximately 19in high, 13in wide and 19in deep), keyboard and graphics writing tablet;

— an under-desk base unit (approximately 26in high, 14in wide and 26in deep).

The PERQ is self-sufficient in that it provides the user with the convenience of a desk-top microcomputer, the power of a minicomputer and the facilities of an interactive graphics terminal – all these features are contained in one stand-alone PERQ workstation, whose base unit contains its CPU, a 1 Mbyte store for the 8-inch floppy disks and a 24 Mbyte 14-inch Winchester fixed disk. The PERQ can of course also be connected to a high-speed local area network (LAN) for access to shared resources and to communicate with other PERQs and other workstations.

IBM 8100 DOSF, DISOSS and PROFS

An electronic office offering from IBM is the IBM 8100/DOSF (Distributed Office Support Facility). DOSF is an IBM 8100-based information system designed for the integration of data processing and text processing. It supports local filing and other electronic office functions. The 8100 can be interfaced over a communications link (SDLC protocol) to an IBM 3705 front end processor and, through that, to an IBM mainframe (eg 370, 303X series). Locally IBM 3270 series office terminals can be attached direct to the 8100, via a local area network, or via communications lines. Other peripherals can be attached to the 8100, such as printers, and the IBM 6670 Information Distributor. The 6670 can communicate with computers and print typewriter-quality originals. It can access and process a wide variety of information. It has a laser printer, receives and transmits documents electronically, processes text and data, and makes convenience copies.

IBM DISOSS (Distributed Office Support System), released in September 1980, and STAIRS (Storage and Information Retrieval System) are available for performing company-wide filing and information retrieval on an IBM mainframe. The addition of two other IBM systems, DIF (Document Interchange Facility) and DCF (Document Composition Facility), gives an integrated system for text, data and publications, available to workstations attached to a local IBM 8100 computer (see also Bibliography, item 4.9). The Norwegian national oil company, Statoil, has installed several IBM 8100 processors in its OA strategy.

At one of the NCC workshops held in 1981 to gather information and views for this book, someone from Cannock-based Compower Ltd, the computer bureau for the National Coal Board and its ancillary companies, supplied the following printout using DCF (see Figure 4.8), with the accompanying comment:

'This reproduction illustrates IBM's Document Composition Facility (DCF) which we (at Compower Ltd) are currently looking at, as part of an overall survey of Word Processing/Mainframe Text requirements. This format is also suitable for printing on our IBM 3800 laser printer using the 90° facility to print vertically on A4 size stationery.'

In Dorking, the Friends Provident Life Office (see Bibliography, item 4.10) became in 1979 one of the first organisations in Europe to install the IBM 3730 Distributed Office Communication System and had increased the number of 3730s to four by the end of 1980. As the work load and the number of IBM 3732 VDU screens increased, there was a progression from the 3730s to 8100/DOSF which provided more power, larger storage, increased function and faster response times.

In November 1981, there were 36 IBM 3732 screens and 12 IBM 3739 daisy wheel printers in use by typists, secretaries and supervisors. The

NCC WORKSHOPS - INFORMATION MANAGEMENT SYSTEMS (IMS).

CONTRIBUTION BY MR. BURNS (COMPOWER LTD). Compower Ltd is
the computer bureau for the National Coal Board and ancillary Companies. Terminals are widely distributed throughout
the NCB organisation with on-line access to several corporate databases covering all main fields of operation. Integration of Office Automation equipment will be linked with
centralised mainframes and IBM's systems network architecture (SNA). The major objectives are to increase productivity of managers and supporting staff consistent with
improving user service and Company profitability.

Progress in various projects is reflected below:-

* many terminals have been installed at pits, other activities and in offices, and this is continuing;

* alternative word processing strategies are being
  assessed;

* much information is currently held on computer
  mainframes and means of exploiting this resource are
  being considered;

* the use of distributed computing (using IBM's SNA), with
  printing and personal computing facilities at local
  sites is being developed;

* ways of improving productivity and effectiveness through
  better management of the information resource are being
  considered (this is a most important aim);

* standard letters, manuals and reports are being considered as word processing applications or for mainframe
  text processing;

* uses of Data Dictionary and of Microfilm techniques are
  being examined;

* IBM Mass Storage systems and their impact on current
  techniques are being considered;

* a large amount of costly photocopying is carried out at
  Cannock; the use of the mainframe computer and the laser
  printer, with its many additional features, is being
  considered as a cheaper and more presentable
  alternative.

Figure 4.8   Illustration of Use of IBM Document Composition Facility

screens were connected to the IBM 8140 (part of the IBM 8100 series),
using the DPCX control software. Although the system has been used
extensively, and very successfully, for word processing, it is also used for
historical archiving of text documents on the IBM 3033 mainframe.
Documents can be accessed and retrieved by users at any time. Future
developments could include the integration of this office system network
to the existing IMS (Information Management System) branch network

so that clerks using IMS screens could:

— access standard letters, retrieve customer details from the IMS database and produce themselves, by answering prompts displayed on the screen for input, high-quality personalised letters;

— extract data from documents prepared on 8100/DOSF and store the data in DP applications programs files on the mainframe.

The 3732 screens could also pass text to the Document Composition Facility in the host computer for the commercial printing of publications.

Word processing is one of the starting points leading to the electronic office and this approach seems most appropriate for the type of office work carried out at Friends Provident Life Office. However, in general, an OA strategy must take account of what the current activities and future needs of office workers are. Three papers in *IBM Systems Journal* are worth reading. The paper, by Engel *et al* (see Bibliography, item 4.11), reports on a prototype OA system designed 'as an experimental learning system to provide managers and professionals with an easy, fast and direct method for handling their business communications'. The paper by Gruhn and Hohl (see Bibliography, item 4.12), discusses a number of computer-assisted aids to office work that have evolved at the IBM Thomas J. Watson Research Centre in Yorktown Heights, New York and provides a preview of possibilities for future office systems based on computers. The third paper, by Gardner (see Bibliography, item 4.13), describes the history of an office system application which served as the basis for a recently-announced (1981) IBM system PROFS (Professional Office System). The electronic office system in use since late 1977 at the Research Centre of the Amoco Production Company in Tulsa, Oklahoma relates to this development.

OTL Information Management Processor (I.M.P.)

In 1981 Office Technology Ltd (OTL) introduced its Information Management Processor (I.M.P.) office system and workstation, which builds office automation features onto a firm base of word processing facilities, and includes the ability to integrate voice communications fully with text, graphics and data. OTL was formed in 1980 to design and manufacture a range of OA products. It is a member company of the independent British Information Technology Limited (ITL) group; its sister companies are the well-known computer manufacturing company Computer Technol-

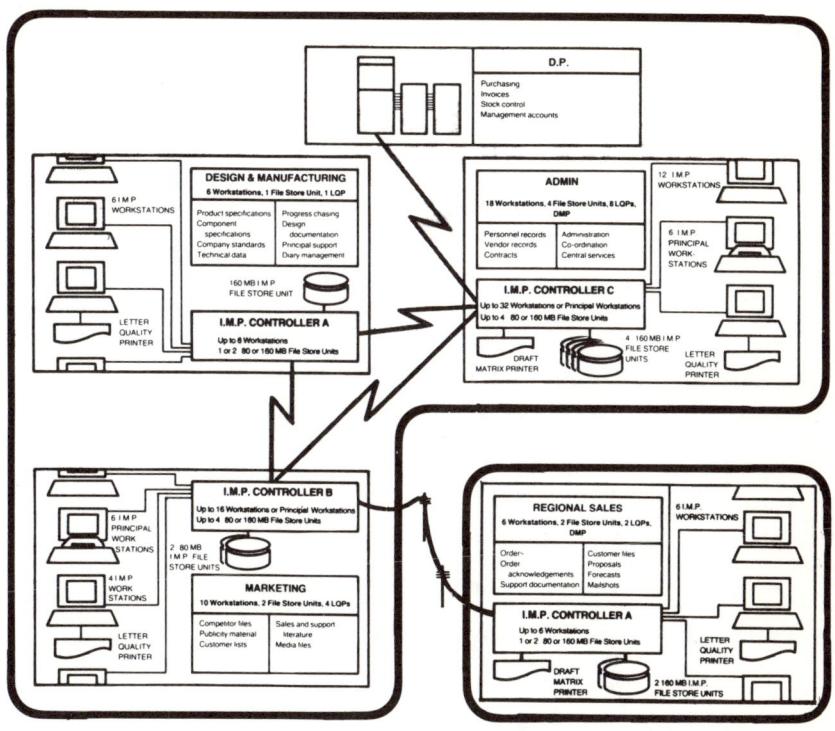

Figure 4.9   OTL I.M.P. Office System Configuration

ogy Limited (CTL), formed in 1966, and Network Technology Limited (NTL), formed in 1981 to supply vendor-independent communications products and systems.

The I.M.P. system has been designed with particular attention paid to the 'Human Factors' elements to make the terminal acceptable to the non-specialist user. Examples of these features are:

— the screen, which displays an exact picture of a paper document, black characters on a white background with attributes such as emboldening and underlining shown as they would be printed with no special control characters;

— the keyboard, which has been designed so that all keys are clearly
  labeled with legible and meaningful legends, and functions are
  easily invoked by a single key depression;

— the filing system, which has been designed to be easy to use as it is a
  hierarchical structure which can mirror the cabinet/drawer/
  folder/wallet indexing used with a conventional paper-based system.

Figure 4.9 illustrates how an I.M.P. system may be used in several
departments of an organisation (such as design and manufacturing, marketing, administration and sales), using the communications features of
the I.M.P. to exchange information between these departments which
may be in different locations. The user workstations (I.M.P Workstations
and I.M.P. Principal Workstations) allow users to integrate:

— text and voice handling;

— word and data processing;

— the creation, storage and distribution of information.

A feature of the I.M.P. Principal Workstation is its voice facilities for:

— sending voice messages;

— dictating and sending dictation to an audio-typist;

— adding voice annotations to drafts and other electronic documents.

The I.M.P. workstation's keyboard contains such useful information
management functions as:

— ANNOTATE   Attaches a voice annotation to any point in a
  document, and finds existing annotations. Allows comments and
  corrections to be added to any document, stored and communicated without writing or typing;

— VIEW DESKTOP/PUT ON DESKTOP   Keeps together your
  current working documents and those you access frequently. Lets
  you select quickly and easily from among frequently-used documents;

— SEND   A single initiation point for all internal and external
  mailing functions. Provides transparent mailing of all documents
  by distribution-list selection;

— IN-TRAY (with built-in light)   Light signals 'message waiting'. If it flashes, the message is urgent (the sender has used PRIORITY SEND);

— MAIL LOG   Keeps track of the information you send out: can be programmed to let you know when all addressees have read your message;

— DIARY (with built-in light)   Stores future appointments and bring-up material: light shows there is an entry under today's date;

— WASTE-BIN 'Shreds' your unwanted information – after a user-defined delay (say, 24 hours) just in case there has been a mistake;

— HELP   Instant information for user guidance. Expansion of prompting information by voice where necessary: no need to clear the screen;

— PERSONAL FILES   Isolates your personal (desk drawer) files from the shared group files. No-one can access these files without your express permission;

— PAGE LAYOUT   Displays a full page at a glance, exactly as it will be printed, for a check on the layout.

Following the I.M.P. launch at the International Business Show in October 1981, a pilot system of two I.M.P. workstations, an I.M.P. controller and two printers was installed in the NCC in March 1982 for NCC's Standardisation Office.

Datapoint Corporation

Datapoint Corporation's products were sold in the UK for many years by Ventek Computers but the company now operates under its own name in the UK as Datapoint UK. It has a well-known local area network called Attached Resource Computer (ARC) which integrates word processing, data processing, electronic mail, facsimile, intelligent printers, business graphics and a digital voice and data switching system (ISX). In November 1981, Datapoint announced that it had received the hundredth UK order for its ARC network.

A product of particular interest from the information management point of view is the Associative Index Method (AIM). This information storage and retrieval product is provided for electronic filing of text and data documents. Filed documents (eg letters, text, lists, price schedules) can be searched for occurrences of a keyboard or keywords, and the names of files containing the keyword(s) can be displayed – or the documents themselves can be displayed.

Its business graphics system includes a workstation with graphics input tablet and stylus, and system controller. The user can produce charts and diagrams without programming. A high resolution (512 x 482) raster scan display can be used to produce 35-mm slides and film prints, as well as 8 x 10 Polaroid prints, colour transparencies (from 16 colours) and printed output. In the electronic office, there is a long-term user requirement for an inexpensive facility for producing hard copy printed output with colour graphics.

An important strategic product is Information Switching Exchange (ISX). This machine is a 'third generation' PBX that can switch voice, data, text and messages over conventional twisted pair wiring within a building and serve as a controller for the integration of office equipment and office functions. It has a Central Switching Unit (CSU) which handles access to remote databases and between Remote Switching Units (RSUs) – which themselves handle local switching access to public or private communications networks and the local interface to the ISX for telephones and workstations. Although ISX is not as yet (November 1982) approved for connection to the BT network, readers should be aware of its existence and facilities, as it illustrates the way in which their communications infrastructure planning could go. The system's switching units are of the 'non-blocking' type.

The company has a database information retrieval system command language called Datascan and is believed to be intending to introduce an electronic filing system based on the cheap, mass storage capability of optical disk technology.

Philips Data Systems Digital Optical Recording

Optical recording of information in digital form on a new recording medium called an optical disk employing advanced technology has been forecast by many writers as having enormous potential for information management systems in the electronic office. One of the first companies to develop this technology is Philips in a joint venture with Control Data; another is the Japanese company Toshiba (see next section) and a third optical disk venture involves the Xerox subsidiary Shugart Associates and the French electronics company Thomson CSF.

Philips Data Systems has developed a 12-inch optical disk, formed from two sides placed back-to-back and making a sealed air sandwich having a lifetime in excess of 10 years. Each side of the disk has a spiral groove which is equivalent to 45,000 concentric tracks each 1.67 microns apart (10^6 microns = 1 metre). Each track is divided into 128 sectors. In each sector 10% of the space forms the sector's address heading, so that sectors can be individually addressed, and 90% of the space is available for the high density recording of data (equivalent to 2 x 10^8 bits/in^2 or 4 x 10^7 bits/cm^2). A total of 1024 bits of user data may be recorded per sector. This makes the capacity of one 12 inch disk about 10^{10} user bits (45,000 tracks x 128 sectors x 1024 user bits x 2 recording surfaces is approximately 1.18 x 10^{10} bits).

The disk's surface is coated with reflective material into which user data is written by melting micron-sized holes on the pregrooved sector area; these holes are detected during reading through reflection variations. Error-free recording is achieved by a combination of an error detection and correction scheme, which adds 20% redundancy to the user data, backed up by a direct read-after-write which leads to an immediate rewrite in another sector if this is ever necessary. Individual sectors can be randomly accessed in a mean access time of 100 ms and the data transfer rate for reading and writing is 2 x 10^6 bit/s. Storage is, of course, of the non-erasable type (unlike magnetic disk and tapes) so that this recording medium has immense potential for archival storage and replacing paper files.

The capacity of a disk is equivalent to half a million typed pages of text. A typed page holds about 2500 characters, which is equivalent to 2 x 10^4 bits (1 character = 8 bits). So 5 x 10^5 pages is equivalent to 10^{10} bits which is the approximate capacity of a disk available for user data, after allowing for sector addresses and error detection. The capacity of an optional disk is also equivalent to 50,000 A4 pages of images, 500 COSATI microfiches, 20 microfilm rolls or 35 magnetic tapes (2400 feet long, recording density 1600 bits per inch).

Design improvements in both magnetic disks and optical disks may be expected to come out of research laboratories in the next year or two. During the next decade during which office automation systems will come into widespread usage, users will be able to employ magnetic disks for the storage of information in the current database, and optical disks for the storage of archived information as well as for image information which is not subject to amendment (eg X-ray, insurance policy and bank cheque images). Gradually all designers of brochures and other material which is today sent through the post will have to bear in mind the ease-of-use requirements of recipients. Many recipients will either store incoming documents on optical disks and throw the original away into the waste paper basket, or will throw the original away without recording it first.

Just as today most jars, tins, bottles and packets sold in food shops contain a bar-coded label, so future brochures and other documents will be designed so that recipients have to do the minimal amount of writing, keying, indexing or annotating in order to store the document on an optical disk in such a way that it can be easily referenced and retrieved. For example, every document might have a small area which contains a menu of keywords which a reader can add to or delete from. When the document is scanned and its image stored on optical disk, an OCR type scan will pick up the keywords and automatically index the document. The Japanese can be expected to play a leading role in this type of research and development.

Toshiba Document Filing System DF-2000 (Tosfile)

An operational electronic document filing system of Toshiba Corporation is the DF-2000 system, also called Tosfile. It was demonstrated to the authors at Toshiba's OA showroom in Tokyo in October 1981.

Tosfile was in 1981 a most impressive facility in terms of progress towards the electronic office. Replicas of up to 10,000 documents can be stored on an optical disk via a laser scanning device. The maximum size for input documents is B4 and the average input speed (excluding document identification input time) is about 8.5 seconds. Each document which is recorded in the system can be identified with six keywords. In a demonstration using an optical disc containing details of some of Tokyo's 10,000 restaurants, the following keywords were used:

—   class (Italian, Japanese etc);

—   location;

—   price range;

—   typical menu;

—   family rooms (this relates to the Japanese culture);

— how many people catered for.

Each keyword can be subdivided into a further 24 classes. Retrieval can be undertaken based on selected keywords and ranges can be specified (eg price range between 10,000 and 20,000 Japanese yen). Recalled documents can be displayed on a screen, where they can be checked before a hard copy printout is obtained. The diameter of an optical disk is 30 cms and the access time (using random access) is about one second. It takes about 4.5 seconds to display a filed document and about 10 seconds to print. Selected parts of a display document can be enlarged by moving a square window over them and the hard copy printout conforms to the Group 3 international facsimile standard (8 by 7.7 dots per square millimetre). The dimensions of the scanner/printer/controller unit are 800 mm (31.4 in) wide by 1080 mm (42.4 in) deep by 980 mm (38.5 in) high (weight 280 Kg (616 lbs)), and of the disk memory unit are 700 mm (27.5 in) wide by 480 mm (18.9 in) deep by 980 mm (38.5 in) high (weight 120 Kg (264 lbs)).

British Telecom X-Stream

In August 1981 BT's new and long-awaited public data service PSS commenced full commercial operation. The 60 pre-operational users started to pay for using the service and those on the waiting list had service made available for them. The number of nodes, or packet switching exchanges (PSEs), increased from 12 to 18 in 1982 and is expected to increase to about 45 in five years. PSS can be assessed through certain Datel services (via the PSTN) or by special lines called 'Datalines'. A wide variety of access speeds is available and PSS provides interworking between terminals operating at different speeds. PSS enables users to connect to similar data networks in other countries via the International Packet Switched Service (IPSS). PSS will also use the X-Stream services, announced by BT in November 1981, not only for digital access to the network but also for internode links.

The four X-Stream services (see Figure 4.10) are MegaStream, KiloStream, SwitchStream and SatStream. The X symbol represents *digital* services (cf System X telephone exchange) and Stream indicates the flow of digital information through the network. The announcement of the X-Stream services represents an extension of the previously announced 'Overlay' network of digital leased circuits, which recognised the unique character and needs of the City business community in London. Further

MegaStream Services (from 1982):

— non-switched
— point-to-point
— MegaStream2 (2 Mbit/s)
    — interface to Monarch and other modern digital PABXs
    — use M2M multiplexer services for speech and data
    — interface to a computer
— Mega Stream8 (8 Mbit/s)
    — in-company private video conferencing
    — other high-speed data transfer applications

KiloStream Services (from 1983):

— non-switched
— point-to-point
— various data applications
— digital local ends for private digital networks
— KiloStream 2.4 (2400 bit/s)
— KiloStream 4.8 (4800 bit/s)
— KiloStream 9.6 (9600 bit/s)
— KiloStream 48 (48 Kbit/s)
— KiloStream 64 (64 Kbit/s)

SwitchStream Services (from 1983 as a pilot):

— circuit switched (but PSS is SwitchStream 1)
— exploit System X exchanges
— interconnection of voice, data, text, graphics and other terminals
— SwitchStreams 2.4, 4.8, 9.6, 48 and 64 are feasible
— Integrated Digital Access service

SatStream Services (from 1984):

— use ECS and Telecom 1 satellites
— small-dish aerials
— cover most of Western Europe
— access to locations difficult to serve terrestrially

Figure 4.10   BT X-Stream Digital Transmission Services

information about X-Stream services may be obtained from BT (see Useful Addresses, item 4.8); a 24-minute colour film about the use of the BT data transmission facilities is also available on free loan from BT (see Useful Addresses, item 4.9).

MegaStream Services ('MegaStreams') are non-switched digital services which became available in London during 1982 and will be provided elsewhere as BT's digital network is extended during 1983. MegaStream 2 will offer a point-to-point digital transmission service at 2 Mbit/s. It may be interfaced directly to modern digital PABXs such as future versions of BT's Monarch. It can also be used for speech and data using MegaStream 2 Multiplexer (M2M) services on a customer's premises. It can also be connected to a computer through a suitable interface for high-speed data transfers. MegaStream 8 offers a point-to-point service at 8 Mbit/s and may be used for video conferencing and other high-speed data transfer applications.

KiloStream services will provide single-channel access to the digital services and will be suitable for various data applications and for providing digital local ends to private digital networks. Leased circuits will allow transmission at rates from 2.4 Kbit/s up to 64 Kbit/s within and between major city centres. KiloStreams 2.4, 4.8, 9.6 and 48 will be provided with an enhanced maintenance service and may be provided quicker than leased circuits are at present because a dedicated network based on the digital transmission network is being provided for them.

SwitchStream services exploit the advanced processor control features of System X exchanges; they interact with the digital network to provide customers with compatible interconnection of voice, data, text, graphics and other terminals. A pilot Integrated Services Digital Network (ISDN) will become operational in London during 1983 to provide the first SwitchStream trial service for selected business users. This will be marketed under the title IDA (Integrated Digital Access).

The fourth X-Stream service is SatStream, which is the name given to communications services based on small-dish aerials mounted on or close to customers' premises used with the European Communications Satellite and the French Telecom 1 satellite. Commercial trials began at the end of 1981 on the Orbital Test Satellite and by 1984 SatStream satellite services will be available for business communications services covering most of Western Europe and will permit customers to implement many applications in advance of full digitalisation of the terrestrial network.

Electronic Publishing and Document Delivery

New technology will cause radical changes in the way in which information is published in the next few years. Books, newspapers and journals will still appear but new technology will change the way in which they are prepared and printed. There will be a shift from hard copy publishing to electronic publishing. This will require changes of attitude and changed working practices by publishers, editors, printers, librarians, abstractors, authors and users. The relevant point is that organisations will be able to receive more and more information from other organisations in electronic form rather than in paper form, not just correspondence and reports, but also published books and technical journals. Therefore organisations must prepare themselves to receive information which is published electronically and to distribute it, or make it available for access, within their organisation.

A consortium was formed in 1981 between Elsevier Science Publishers, Pergamon Press Ltd (UK) and Springer Verlag of Heidelberg, West Germany to prepare for entry into this new market with the aim of creating a full text database of documents from which simple articles could be produced on demand.

This move followed from a study of the demand for copies and loans of single articles, often selected after an on-line search of a database, and a survey of existing and emerging technology. To be viable and successful, any service which might start up in 1984 or 1985 would depend upon publishers co-operating by placing their publications onto an electronic system.

Allied to electronic publishing is the concept of electronic document delivery. There are in existence many on-line databases allowing users from their desk top workstation to access files of document titles and abstracts, browse and select specific items. These can be displayed and printed at the user's office, but it may be cheaper, although slower, to request copies of selected titles and abstracts to be printed at the host computer and posted as a letter. The user can then request photocopies of the actual articles from the computer centre, national or local library, NCC Information Service, or elsewhere.

On-line electronic document delivery completes the final link in the chain between information originator and end user. A system which has been proposed by the Compagnie d'Information Générale de Liège

(CIGL, a Euronet-DIANE host) and Correlative Systems International (CSI) is illustrated in Figure 4.11. Full journal articles, photographs and diagrams could be delivered electronically from a library direct to a user's office.

   Documents could be identified by an on-line search, over Euronet-DIANE for example, in the normal way and orders passed to an image system which is the link between the mass storage and the on-line network. Documents could be read by an optical scanner at the rate of 2000

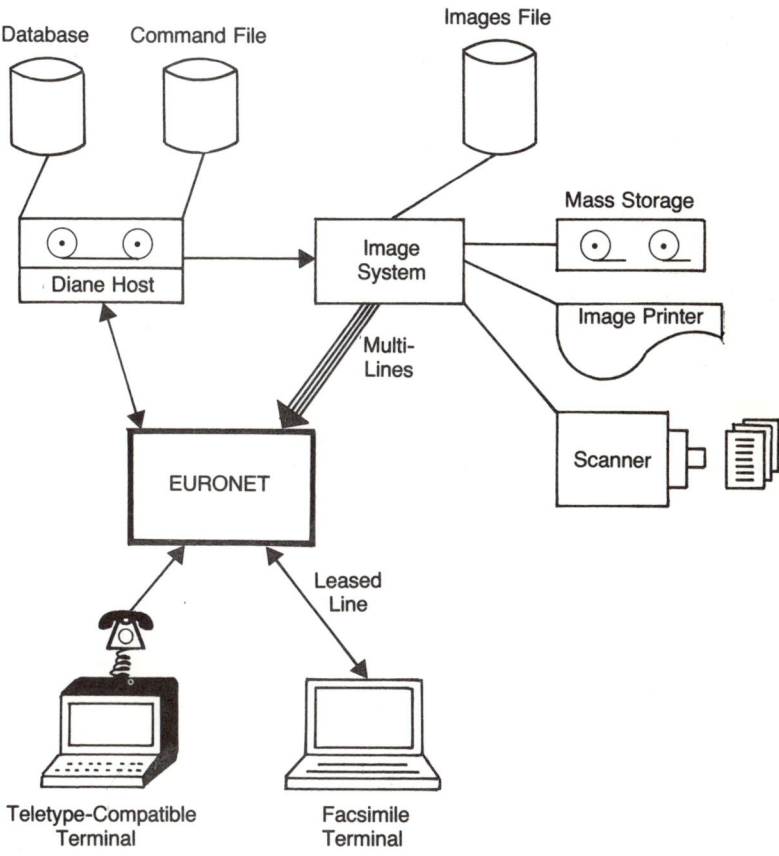

Figure 4.11   Electronic Document Delivery System

A4 pages an hour and stored digitally on a mass storage optical disk system. Selected documents could be transmitted, during network off-peak periods, at rates up to 1000 A4 pages per hour and finally delivered to a user's document delivery terminal where a document is received and printed at high-speed on a facsimile receiver.

The CEC is carrying out a programme for the development of electronic publishing and document delivery systems to discover whether the electronic delivery of full text documents to users is cost-effective and acceptable. It has been suggested that a target cost to users of 1 EAU (NB 1 European Unit of Account was worth about $1 US in August 1981) for a facsimile page and 0.5 EAU for a teletex transmitted page should be aimed at, although unit prices for the delivery of electronic documents will depend on overall market demand. In the UK the National Physical Laboratory (NPL) and PIRA, the Department of Industry's research association for the paper and board, printing and package industries, have carried out a joint project definition study for Project HERMES and prepared a report for the Department of Industry. HERMES is a proposed electronic document viewing and delivery network which will interconnect teletex terminals. Users will be able to input information, store and edit it, and move it to other workstations on the network. Terminals will be located in libraries and information centres. A central computer will hold a database of documents operated by the Publishers Association, and will have a front-end teletex interface. Announcements about books and journals can be sent through the network to the user terminals, which can be used to retrieve documents from the database.

The proposed system could be enhanced for documents with graphical diagrams, with the text characters coded in the normal way and the graphics handled by facsimile methods. (The disadvantages of using facsimile methods only are that too much storage would be needed and that it would not be possible for the text part of the document to be edited, eg one could not move a paragraph from one document into a report one was preparing.) If successful, project HERMES could pave the way for a national value-added service, publicly and/or privately operated, with documents containing a mix of text and graphics being stored on optical disk and delivered electronically to teletex-compatible multifunction workstations.

5 Strategic Issues

INTRODUCTION

It is assumed that the reader (having also read the companion volume, see Bibliography, item 1.3):

— is aware of the need for the development of a corporate OA strategy rather than an *ad hoc* approach by individual user departments;

— feels confident about the right way for his organisation to undertake the OA strategic planning process;

— understands the various strategy options which may be appropriate;

— understands the various types of message (and EMS), and the various types of information (and IMS);

— understands the relevant strategic issues and design considerations for an EMS strategy, within the overall OA strategy, and how to address them;

— wants guidance about the relevant strategic issues and design considerations for an IMS strategy, within the overall OA strategy, and how to address them.

This chapter and the next discuss the last point in this list. This chapter gives an overview from the points of view, first of the user organisation and then of the supplier organisation, and goes on to consider what we believe are the important strategic issues.

THE USER ORGANISATION

Many studies have shown that the office is under-capitalised compared with agriculture and the factory, ie the per capita expenditure on machinery and equipment to help the office worker is many times less the expenditure on agricultural workers and people employed in factories. However, this is not, in isolation, a reason for taking any action. These studies also show that productivity has risen much faster in agriculture and industry than in offices and that, in offices, costs are rising faster than productivity. The first major reason why organisations should want to investigate if and how new office technology can help is in order to:

— control costs and improve productivity.

In Japan, during the decade 1968 to 1978, investment had raised productivity in agriculture by 185%, in industry by 90%, and in offices by 4%. From 1975 to 1979, Japanese labour costs in offices increased by 7%, while the costs of communications, electronics and storage dropped by 10%, 20% and 40% respectively. The use of OA is perceived as the means of turning round labour costs from a 7% increase to a 7% decrease.

At a UK seminar to launch IBM's office systems strategy we were told that IBM must be a user of OA systems: projections showed an increased throughput of work in IBM offices which could not be handled by a proportional increase in the number of office employees if the company's products were to continue to be competitively priced. This gives the second major reason (which is a more emphatic restatement of the first):

— to remain competitive and survive.

One non-manufacturing organisation, which sells computing services both within the group of companies of which it is part and externally, felt that the most compelling reason for it to use OA was to improve its ability to respond (to external inquiries, to internal decisions, to events, to opportunities etc) by improving its communications through EMS and its information handling through IMS. (NB Like NCC and other computing services organisations it also wants hands-on experience of new technology so that its advice to others is based upon first-hand experience and so that it can be seen to be practising what it preaches.) This gives the third major reason:

— to be more responsive.

During the last five years or so in the UK, there has been an emphasis on word processing and on its cost benefits and increased productivity in respect of copy typists. Word processing has an important place in the electronic office: it will be several years before OCR and voice recognition systems are capable of, and cost-effective for, interpreting natural handwriting and natural speech. But to-day's junior copy typists should not be surprised if their grandchildren, if not their children, take a handwritten document out of the in-tray or listen to an author's recorded text and speak its contents into a word processor which has been programmed to understand its user's way of speaking English.

Word processors have been emphasised as amongst the first products available for the electronic office. Again, from an OA strategy point of view, this is all right because WP is a reasonable strategy option for entering into the electronic office migration path. However, the authors feel most strongly that an OA strategy must change emphasis and be concerned primarily with managers and professionals, and must be concerned more with value-added benefits and less with cost savings. This requires a significant degree of change of attitude by many UK managers and investment decision-makers; it also requires much hard work by corporate OA strategy planners who have to identify opportunities for value-added benefits. This gives the fourth major reason:

—   to provide value-added benefits.

Some readers may not be familiar with this concept and an example will illustrate:

—   what is meant;

—   how it differs from a cost-benefit investment attitude;

—   how important it is.

A UK manufacturing organisation sells its products to shops and other wholesale and retail outlets for resale to the public. An in-house private viewdata system was developed and implemented in order to provide salesmen with better information in the expectation that this would help them to secure more orders.

Sales did increase by 25% in those geographical regions (about one in every three) which made use of this IMS. It was estimated that 5% of this figure was due directly to the use of the system (ie to the convenient and immediate access by the sales force to up-to-date information about discounts, special promotions, stock levels, delivery schedules, etc), and

— to control costs and improve productivity;

— to remain competitive and survive;

— to be more responsive;

— to provide value-added benefits;

— to support better-quality decision-making and better-quality creative work.

Figure 5.1   Strategic Reasons for Using OA Systems

the remaining 20% to other factors. The annual running cost of the system
was £100,000 and the original annual sales figure was £10 million. So the
cost of using the system is about 1% of turnover (plus the development
costs which it is hoped to recover through the sale of the IMS), while its
benefit in those regions where it was used is about 5% (five times as
much). Probably in most UK companies today, and very likely in most
local authorities which are operating within cash limits and no-growth
policies, cost savings and not value-added benefit is the investment criterion. If this organisation had thought likewise, this IMS would not have
been developed, implemented or used, the benefits from the increased
sales would not have been gained, and instead of gaining a competitive
edge over rivals its existing market share could have been eroded.

A fifth major reason, a refinement of the fourth reason, emphasises the
importance of meeting the needs of managers and professionals (who
should conceive new products and prevent an organisation from beaver-
ing away on a path that leads nowhere). This reason emphasises the need:

—   to support better-quality decision-making and better-quality crea-
    tive work.

These five reasons are highlighted in Figure 5.1.

The strategy should seek to match up:

—   the applications (eg lists of names, addresses, and telephone num-
    bers of people and organisations; diary management; tickler file;
    internal telephone directory and room allocation directory);

— the functions (eg filing; search and retrieval; interpersonal communication; archiving of information; generation of documents; information distribution; updating of electronic documents);

— the users (eg managers; professionals; technical personnel; secretaries; keyboard operatives; filing clerks);

— the forms of information (ie text; data; graphics; image; voice);

— the electronic office solutions (eg electronic mail; private viewdata systems; word processing; electronic filing; multifunction workstations; value-added network services (VANS); digital PABXs; Euronet-DIANE; Prestel Gateway; local area networks (LANs); British Telecom's X-Stream digital transmission services; optical disks).

It should identify appropriate and cost-effective migration paths and milestones and be able to introduce new solutions as technological developments (in chips, in optical disks, in optical fibres, in communications satellites, etc) lead to new products (eg multifunction workstations, private digital exchanges) and new services (eg VANS operated by British Telecom and private organisations).

The operational performance of organisations is being impaired by the nuisances of:

— paper pollution;

— information overload.

Paper is a nuisance because:

— its storage consumes space; space is a valuable resource; space should be occupied by people and machines which create wealth and add value to an organisation; in many organisations paper files occupy space out of all proportion to their cost-effectiveness; organisations should monitor how much capacity in offices (ie how many cubic yards of space, and how many square yards of floor space) is used by paper (including the paper storerooms of unused A4 paper, envelopes, continuous stationery, and archived paper files, as well as current paper files) and seek to reduce this month by month, year by year; much office accommodation is devoted to paper files, of which many individual sheets of paper are infrequently or never accessed. Several organisations have introduced

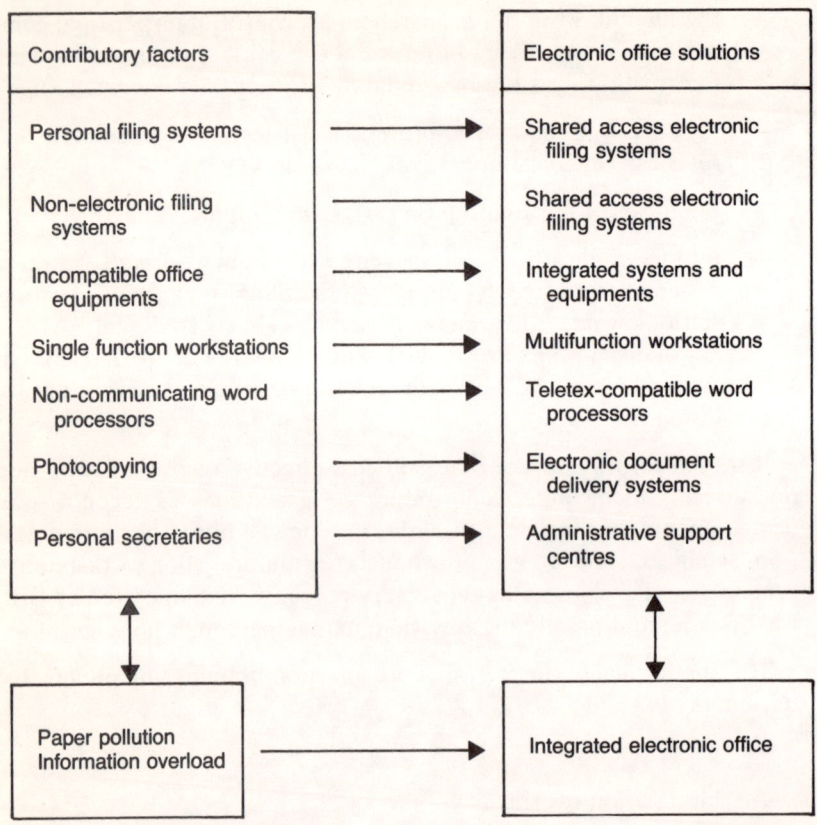

**Figure 5.2   Paper Pollution and Information Overload – The Escape
Routes**

microfiche and microfilm facilities to conserve space and many are
looking forward to the availability of optical disk-based document
filing systems;

—   its handling (filing, access and retrieval) consumes manpower;
manpower is another valuable resource; in the electronic office
there will be a migration from paper filing to electronic filing – and
one of the purposes of the IMS strategy is to plan for this migration
over a number of years; at present, an enormous amount of

information in paper files is wasted, because people who need to use it either are not aware of its existence (and consequently duplicate effort in obtaining this information) or cannot justify the time that would be spent in searching for and retrieving it.

In many organisations there is a realisation that paper pollution exists, that something must be done about it and that IMS provide the solution. In many more organisations, there is a lack of awareness, which this book and other outputs from NCC's office systems work programme can try to overcome, and/or a stubbornly-held attitude that paper is a friendly medium and will continue to be widely used because it always has been. We believe that this attitude, although understandable, is not in the best interests of organisations wishing to survive into the 1990s.

Information overload simply refers to the fact that there is a growing amount of internally generated information and an even larger amount of information generated outside the organisation which managers and professionals should know about and refer to in their work. Electronic office systems provide the only way in which people can be put in touch with, search, access and retrieve large amounts of useful information. Organisations who do not use IMS will find that their operations will tend to become uncompetitive and irrelevant. Figure 5.2 illustrates a number of factors contributing to paper pollution and information overload and how these can be overcome in the integrated electronic office.

There are a number of driving forces, in addition to the strategic reasons listed in Figure 5.1, providing a climate in which user organisations are being pushed towards OA and also a number of obstacles. These are shown in Figure 5.3.

THE SUPPLIER ORGANISATION

In the course of gathering information and views relating to OA strategy planning in preparation for this book and the companion volume (see Bibliography, item 1.3), more than 70 organisations have been visited during 1980 and 1981 in the UK, Europe, USA and Japan, several of these visits were to suppliers. The primary purpose of these visits was:

— to discover what the suppliers perceive to be the relevant strategic issues and design considerations which users should address in their OA strategy planning and how they (the suppliers) relate their products and marketing strategies to these perceptions.

Driving forces
— technological developments leading to better products and services

      — multifunction workstations

      — value-added network services

      — local area networks

      — digital exchanges

      — British Telecom's X-Stream digital transmission services,
        Prestel, PSS, etc.

— government initiatives (eg IT82, pilot electronic offices, liberalisation of BT monopoly)

— awareness of the Japanese threat to capture export markets

— perception by some trades unions that new technology must be
  introduced into offices (and factories)

Obstacles

— resistance to change

— feelings of insecurity about the consequences of change upon jobs

— user unfriendly workstations and information retrieval and filing
  procedures

— lack of standards (eg for local area networks, for information
  retrieval command languages, for open systems interconnection)

— incompatibility (non-interoperability) of electronic office offerings
  from different suppliers

— cost-savings based investment attitudes

— resistance by some trades unions to the introduction of new technology

**Figure 5.3   The Integrated Electronic Office – Driving Forces and
Obstacles**

Secondary purposes were:

— to learn about the supplier's products;

— to gain an insight into the short-term and longer-term research and product development strategies of the suppliers.

In the competition for markets, it is likely that there will be more suppliers and products than the market can stand. The market for office systems products will be simply huge. This will attract investment away from the declining industries and into new technology – into research, development and marketing of products for the information society into which we are currently being transformed. Nevertheless the market place will become saturated and many supplier organisations will not survive, or will merge with others, or will restrict their attention to specialised markets or particular countries. Those organisations who are likely to survive and succeed are those who are:

— backed by strong investment;

— have access to leading-edge research;

— understands users' problems and needs;

— have products which lead to the integrated electronic office, eg machines which can communicate through local area networks and intelligent private digital exchanges with machines supplied by other manufacturers and which perform different information processing tasks.

There are different types of supplier organisation in the OA market place:

— mainframe suppliers (eg IBM, ICL);

— minicomputer suppliers (eg Datapoint, Computer Technology);

— communications organisations (eg Plessey, Racal);

— office products suppliers (eg Xerox, Gestetner);

— specialist OA suppliers (eg Xionics, Office Technology Limited);

— consultants, eg NCC, Eosys (NB this company was known until March 1982 as Urwick Nexos), Logica, Communications Studies and Planning, EIU (Economist Intelligence Unit) Informatics Ltd;

— systems suppliers (eg Langton Information Systems);

— British Telecom.

Many suppliers have taken steps (through acquisitions, mergers, forming associated companies, etc), to broaden their base into those technologies where they may be weak. Just as user organisations have different investment attitudes, so different marketing approaches by suppliers
have been detected. In the West (UK, Western Europe, USA), one finds
amongst many suppliers a strong and growing conviction that their products should:

— integrate together into electronic systems various office activities
  which hitherto have been performed on different machines and
  which have incurred delays, physical movement of documents and
  time-consuming (and therefore expensive) manual processes;

— improve the ease and speed with which people can communicate
  with each other;

— enable managers and professionals to access up to date and relevant information quickly and easily (without also retrieving irrelevant information during the search), or, to put it another way, that
  their products should:

  — add value;

  — provide opportunity hours for more creative work;

  — provide time compression.

But one also finds a very strongly held conviction, no doubt a hangover
from the recent marketing strategy for word processors, that OA systems
should increase productivity and cut operational costs. Indeed two major
suppliers take the approach that users must restructure their office support services by forming administrative support centres for two reasons:

— to obtain the benefits from putting on each office worker's desk
  the multifunction workstation which is appropriate to the needs,
  an organisation must have already introduced the right organisation restructuring;

— the savings in support staff, stationery, etc, can justify the expenditure on the OA systems.

It is worthwile discussing this reasoning. Because information systems,

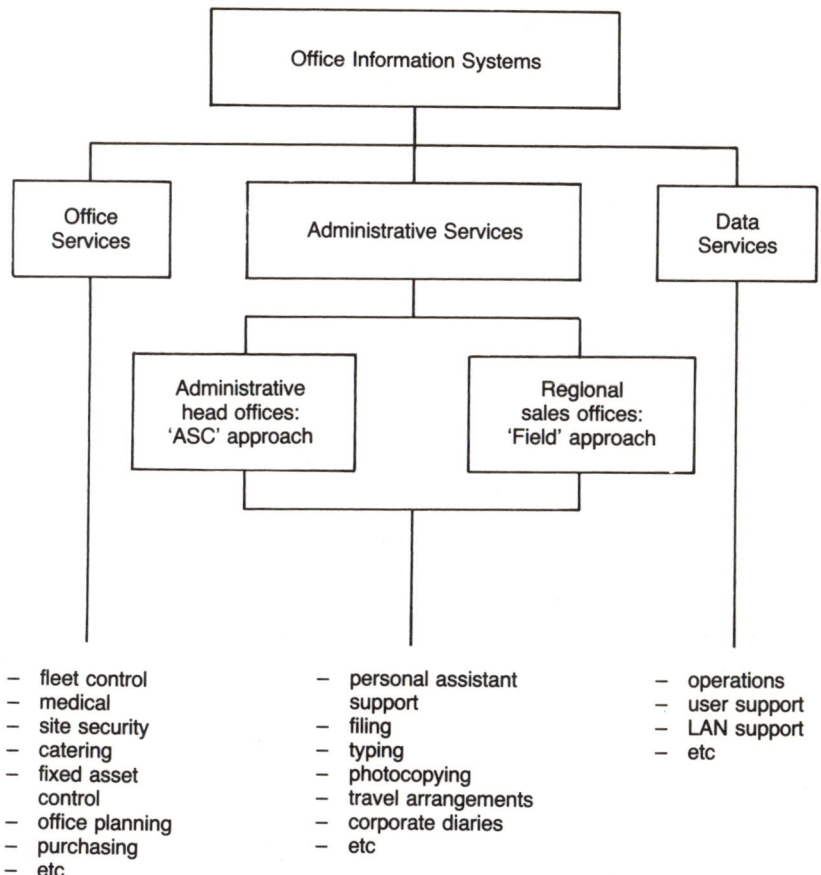

Figure 5.4   An Organisational Structure for the Electronic Office

telecommunications, word processing, local area networking, information storage and retrieval, etc, overlap so much at a user organisation's site, it makes sense to integrate responsibility for all of these into a single post, say Manager of Office Information Systems. This person is responsible for three main functions (see Figure 5.4):

— Office Services;

— Administrative Services;

— Data Services.

Office Services personnel use machines such as those shown in Figure 5.5 (which also shows the machines used by personnel in Administrative Services, and those used by personnel supported by Data Services). The Administrative Support Centre approach brings together into one unit (an ASC or secretariat) the secretaries and typists who previously supported the departments now supported by the ASC. (NB An amended approach, the 'Field' approach, has been developed for regional sales

---

Office services personnel use:

— telex machines

— facsimile machines

— franking machines

— photocopying machines (for bulk photocopying)

Administrative services personnel use:

— word processors

— intelligent printers

— electronic typewriters

— computer terminals

— office copiers

— telex- and teletex-compatible workstations

Data services personnel support managerial/professional users of:

— managerial workstations

— professional workstations

— personal desk-top microcomputers

— local area networks

Figure 5.5   Deployment of Office Equipment

offices where personnel are out of the office selling for much of their time.) It should be noted that there are moves (eg telex switches, teletex) for text messages to be sent electronically from desk to desk, or mailbox to mailbox, rather than post room to post room.

An ASC study computes the ratio, before restructuring into ASC, of 'the number of personnel needing support to the number giving support', and estimates the improved ratio, which ASC restructuring should bring, of 'the number of personnel needing support to the number of personnel in the ASC'. The benefits of an ASC are that:

— the ASC can give a more effective and responsive service (eg there is back-up if someone in the ASC is away, whereas in the conventional structure some activities in a department are disrupted when the departmental secretary is away);

— the departmental line manager is relieved of the burden of administration of the secretarial resource, does not have to worry about what to do during periods of non-availability and does not have to use 'temps';

— the professional or knowledge worker is given better support because of the improved arrangements for the sharing of work between ASC personnel;

— ASC personnel do not experience periods of boring under-utilisation or of being under unreasonable pressure to meet deadlines;

— word processing can be introduced;

— a reduction in the number of support staff;

— a reduction in the number of typing machines.

We agree that this restructuring is an essential precondition which should be satisfied before full OA benefits are attained by users. It seems to us to be analogous to the views expressed to us in several discussions:

— do not computerise a badly designed system (or do not automate the existing mess);

— eliminate rigour.

Figure 5.6 tabulates the results of eleven ASC studies carried out by a supplier organisation. Two of these were for customers and the others

Site	Ratio ASC users: ASC personnel		Headcount saving	
	Before study	After implementation	Number of persons	%
1	4.0	4.5	12	10
2	4.8	5.8	7	20
3	7.6	9.2	5	17
4	4.4	5.9	9	25
5	6.9	6.6	NOT IMPLEMENTED	
6	6.6	9.0	5	26
7	6.1	7.4	3	18
8	7.3	9.0	3	19
9	7.2	11.3	9	36
Customer 1	3.4	5.0	31	31
Customer 2	2.3	3.1	6	24

Figure 5.6   Results of Headcount Savings Achievable by ASC Restructuring

were for head office sites in different European countries. In one instance, the study was not implemented; the special circumstances being that in the country concerned there was a widespread use of part-time support staff, so support staff turned up to work when there was work to do and stayed at home or went home when there was no work to do.

The benefits (actual and potential) which the supplier organisation had found (as at June 1981) based on the implementation of ASCs and the introduction of word processing at sites throughout the world are shown in Figure 5.7 and Figure 5.8 shows the benefits achievable at the supplier's UK headquarters site in London.

In these cases, the supplier is referring to a first step along the migration path to the electronic office. Support staff, not creative staff, are being

Type of benefit	Degree of benefit
— savings of secretarial headcount:	13%
— staff turnover rate reduced	37%
— use of temporary staff reduced:	68%
— stationery costs reduced:	30%
— attitude survey of staff:	
prefer to have ASCs:	74%
prefer not to have ASCs:	10%*
undecided:	16%
— increased opportunity hours for managers (who had not previously had a personal secretary) and professionals:	12% (1980 fig.)
— good training for supplier's sales and sales support staff:	unquantifiable
— better career development opportunites for ASC personnel:	unquantifiable

* none of the managers who previously had a personal secretary expressed this preference

Figure 5.7 Benefits Achievable from ASCs and Word Processing – Worldwide, June 1981

redeployed into ASCs. Some are not required and the headcount is reduced by natural wastage; the remainder are more productively employed because work is scheduled better, because they have word processors and because filing is centralised. Following this the supplier developed, and introduced in the UK early in 1982, its next batch of OA products – workstations for managers and professionals and a local area network. It seems to us that those products will have to be marketed with a greater emphasis on added-value benefits to the users and a lesser emphasis on cost savings and increased productivity. Opportunity hours should certainly be created, but more importantly the quality of the user's work should be improved.

— 124 secretarial staff reduced to 112 ASC staff (57 Administrative
Assistants, 40 Correspondence Secretaries and 15 Administrative
Clerks) deployed in 15 ASCs

— 124 typing machines (electric typewriters) replaced by 50 typing
machines (word processors); 40 word processors allocated to Correspondence Secretaries and 10 more also needed

— creation of centralised filing systems operated by ASC personnel

— elimination of all 'permanent' temporary staff

**Figure 5.8   Benefits Achieved from ASCs and Word Processing –
Supplier's UK Headquarters**

	Japan	USA	West Germany	UK
1970	1.1	4.9	0.7	2.6
1975	1.9	8.5	4.7	4.2
1978	2.2	6.0	4.4	6.0
1979	2.1	5.8	3.8	5.6
1980	2.0	7.2	3.8	7.3
March 1981	2.5	7.3	5.2	10.1

Note: an alternative view suggests that if jobseekers and part-time workers are taken into
account, the overall employment scene may not be that different to the situation obtaining in
many Western countries.

Figure 5.9   Unemployment Trends – Percentage Unemployed

In Japan, we found a rather different attitude towards marketing OA
products by suppliers – an almost single-minded attitude towards automating any process which can be automated (in office and factory). This
can release manpower for redeployment. In Japan new technology is
generally seen as the means of creating employment – not as the agent
which puts people into the dole queue and which causes boredom, frustration and helplessness. There is a strong OA fever in the streets and in
the media; the man-in-the-street appears to be very enthusiastic about
OA.

The definition of unemployment may not be the same in different countries but the statistics in Figure 5.9 highlight a major difference between Japan, the UK and other countries. In the future, Japan's unemployment figures may not always be so low in absolute terms and relatively vis-a-vis other countries, but it seems that by moving investment quickly and positively into the 'sunrise' industries, Japan has acted sensibly and has created jobs – a fact officially noted early in 1982 by UK Secretary of State for Industry, Mr Patrick Jenkin, and acted upon in the UK Government's 1982 Budget.

In many Japanese companies, a harmonious and co-operative spirit between management, employees and unions is encouraged. Efforts are made to consult and reach a consensus. Employees, at least in many of the large companies, do not fear office technology, because they expect to be retained, redeployed and retrained. OA is seen as doing for offices what robots are doing in Japanese factories – make Japanese products more competitive and Japanese organisatons more efficient. The availability of redeployed manpower can be represented as a valuable resource which will allow an organisation to move into new areas of work ahead of competitors.

Japanese OA suppliers have strategies which on paper seem sound – leading to the integrated electronic office. Their products include:

— facsimile machines;

— plain paper copiers;

— Japanese language word processors (and some English language word processors, eg the Toshiba EW-100);

— personal computers (eg the NEC PC-8000);

— small business computers (eg the Toshiba T200);

— Toshiba Tosfile DF-2000 Document Filing System;

— Hitachi Stored Program Control DX-30 Digital PABX and HDX10 Digital Telephone Exchange;

— Nippon Electric Company's proposed integrated electronic PBX.

Some comments on the strategies of Japanese OA suppliers are interesting. Hitachi is well known in the West for its mainframes particularly (and we were most impressed by a large Hitachi installation at the

University of Tokyo which we were kindly shown by Professor Hisao Yamada). This company made the following points:

— EDP systems handle about 35% of an organisation's information processing/management requirements; the OA products will focus on the human being-associated informal information processes such as forecasting and writing proposals;

— whereas EDP systems involve coded, numerical data, office work is difficult to formalise for typically it involves the handling of documental, non-coded information;

— office tasks are generally performed by people with little or no computer experience, but these people are an integral part of the information management process; therefore OA systems must be designed to involve the human being if they are to be implemented and operated successfully with a minimum of user resistance; hence Hitachi's slogan: HUMANICATION;

(NB HUMANICATION = HUMAN + compunICATION
COMPUNICATION = COMPUter + commuNICATION)

— OA systems should increase productivity and add value, but not be responsible for employees losing their jobs; fifth-generation inference machines are a decade away, so human thinking will not be replaced by computers yet; OA must create more time for creative thinking and must provide tools to support that creative thinking;

— OA systems must be very reliable;

— activity analysis schedules should identify within a user organisation the shadow functions or non-productive time for different categories of employee, ie the time which is not being spent to add value; OA systems create opportunity hours by reducing or eliminating the constituent components of the total non-productive time and this opportunity time can be used for creative work and for adding value to the organisation; examples of shadow functions are:

    — unsuccessful telephone calls (if 72% of business calls do not connect first time for one reason or another, then to make 16 successful calls requires ($16 \div 0.28$) = 57 calls of which 41 are wasted calls, representing say 20 minutes); this shadow function can be eliminated by electronic mail;

- time spent in searching someone else's files for a paper document, making a photocopy of it and filing it in one's own paper filing system; the solution for this shadow function is shared-access electronic filing with a user-friendly access and retrieval procedure;

- optical disks for document filing and retrieval hold great promise for saving space in offices and for helping users to access information.

The Mitsubishi Research Institute is not itself an OA supplier, but Japan's second largest think-tank (with 418 professional research staff, 42 administrative and support staff, 7 senior management and a large CRAY 1 mainframe front-ended by a duplex IBM S370/168 configuration). There we learned about the Japanese business culture, including the 'enterprise union' structure, consensus decision-making and 'nemawashi' communication – which adds up to Japanese organisations welcoming change through OA. We also learned about abbreviations and slogans. If the survival of organisations depends upon investment in OA and if investment decisions depend not only upon managers being able to justify expenditure and change but also upon employees welcoming change, then OA popularisation may not be as trivial as it seems at first sight. (Perhaps Japanese efforts in this area are more effective and enduring than the UK's IT82.)

Abbreviations, which can be seen as helping the man-in-the-street to relate to OA, include:

- OA (office automation);

- offucom (office computer);

- worpro (word processor);

- micom (microcomputer);

- persacom (personal computer);

- fax (facsimile);

- ppc (plain paper copier).

Slogans include:

- 'HUMANICATION' (Hitachi);

- 'the creativity office' (Matsushita);

— 'better information, better future' (Mitsubishi);

— 'new life now' and 'new business now' (Sharp);

— 'PRESTO' and 'CREATE' (Sharp), where:

P = paper, for the efficient use of paper
R = records, for the efficient filing
  of records
E = energy-saving
S = space-saving
T = time-saving
O = organisation, for simplified
  efficient organisation,
and
C = comfortable
R = reliable
E = easy
A = activity
T = taste
E = expert.

These two slogans sum up very succinctly what IMS strategic issue and design considerations are all about; PRESTO for the strategic issues and CREATE for the design considerations. These slogans also convey the impression of quick and convenient access to information, and aids to more creative working.

At present, on-line databases are generally under-developed in Japan and much of Japan's on-line information retrieval is done via USA databases – which incurs expensive telephone usage. (A Japanese organisation called Nikkei provides a prominent on-line information system called NEEDS-IR.) The reason for this under-development is that there is a text entry bottleneck, which the invention of the Japanese language word processor by Toshiba in 1979 – there are now more than twenty manufacturers of Japanese language word processors – will help to overcome, and which voice recognition will probably affect dramatically.

At Sharp Corporation, points made included:

— some products are aimed at personal use, eg:

— portable data entry machines;

- pocket calculators (solar photovoltaic cells version invented in 1980);

- personal computers;

- language translation machines (invented 1979);

- single line display portable word processors;

and others are made for corporate use, eg:

- desk-top data-entry machines;

- office computers;

- Japanese language word processors (and the WD-7000 English language word processor);

- facsimile machines;

- copiers.

- in Japanese offices, letters are handwritten and transmitted by facsimile; girls do not work as typists but as clerk-workers doing rewrites of annotated handwritten documents (this is a simplification);

- stand-alone word processors will be replaced by teletex-compatible communicating word processors which can be linked to computers to provide electronic filing and data processing facilities;

- office computers and personal computers can be integrated with facsimile;

- the company showed a most impressive film of research and development in its laboratories and an OA migration strategy with milestones in 1984, 1987 and 1990 which suggested that this company could become an OA force in a few years' time.

The highlight of the visit to Toshiba Corporation's showroom in the Minato-ku, district of Tokyo, was the demonstration of the Tosfile Document Filing System, Japan's first optical disk filing system. Toshiba also developed Japan's first computer in 1954 (with Tokyo University), Japan's first commercial computer in 1957 and Japan's first Japanese language word processor, JW-10, in 1979. We learned of a breakdown of the office work of managers and professionals from data gathered by

A	Communication of information	23.4%
A1	— telephone calls	6.9%
A2	— face-to-face meetings	7.5%
A3	— conferences	5.9%
A4	— dispatching and distribution	3.1%
B	Creating and editing information	31.3%
B1	— consideration/decision-making	9.6%
B2	— reading	6.1%
B3	— writing/computing	15.6%
C	Retrieving and editing information	12.6%
D	Duplicating and printing	11.8%
D1	— duplicating	4.6%
D2	— typing	2.3%
D3	— rewriting by hand	4.9%
E	Travel	5.6%
F	Other	15.3%
	TOTAL	100.0%

Figure 5.10   Breakdown of Office Work in Japanese Offices

JBMA (Japan Business Machine Makers Association) (see Figure 5.10).

The visit to the Matsushita OA Centre (this organisation's products are known in the West under the names National and Panasonic) in the Chuo-ku district of Tokyo left one impressed by the range and quality of their facsimile machines; over 200 products have been developed for office documents, photographs, colour photographs, newspaper pages, finger-prints, weather maps, weather satellites and colour enlarging printing. Despite this major concern in facsimile, there was a clear understanding of the importance of employing office technology to free people for creative work, embraced in the slogan 'the creativity office' and that the integrated electronic office will follow from:

— advances in VLSI chip technology;

— multifunction workstations;

— local area networks;

— gateways to national and international communications networks and value added network services.

Some eye-catching devices were:

— a handheld computer (RL-H1000) contained in a portable slim executive-style briefcase and weighing 11 lbs which was produced for export to the USA market, but not (as at November 1982) approved by NTT for connection to the Japanese PSTN. This handheld computer, which itself weighs only $1\frac{1}{2}$ lbs, was launched on the European market at the Hanover Fair in April 1982 at a basic price of £350;

— pocket terminals (VC-321 and VC-311) for use as stand-alone calculators or as remote telephone data entry devices (one end of a cord attachment plugs into the terminal and the other fits on to the telephone speaker);

— a facsimile machine (UF-215), capable of operating to CCITT Group 3 standard as well as at 9600 bit/s over telephone lines and taking 15 seconds to print an A4 page;

— a portable lightweight facsimile machine (claimed to be the lightest facsimile machine in the world) for sending black-and-white photographs (FAX 201-M).

There were also small business computers, personal computers, Japanese language word processors and plain paper copiers.

Matsushita also have:

— a facsimile automatic message switching system (FAMSS);

— PIP (patent information processor), a system which retrieves, displays and produces hard copy information from a central computer data bank;

— an on-line data entry facsimile system (ODEFAS), a 'third generation' facsimile machine which uses OCR input, is computer controlled and is claimed to be the first facsimile system in the world with an information processing capability;

— integrated facsimile/OCR equipment; alphanumeric information is collected at remote sites on preformatted documents and transmitted by facsimile to the computer centre where it is read by OCR (about 55 Katakana characters can be recognised);

— a microfile facsimile system; 60 frames of information are held on a microfiche card so that 420,000 frames of information are stored in a carousel of microfiche cards; the user first searches a paper directory (index) to find the co-ordinates of the required frame of information; these co-ordinates are entred into the operator's console and the frame is retrieved automatically and displayed on the screen; a facsimile copy can be obtained locally and at remote sites via the telephone network if desired. There were apparently no plans at the time of our visit to provide a computer-aided keyword indexing system which would seem to be very desirable from the points of view of ease of use and ease of index updating.

CONVERGING TECHNOLOGIES AND INTEGRATION

An OA strategy for a user organisation must take account of the converging technologies of:

— computing;

— office systems;

— telecommunications.

This is due to advanced technological research and developments in:

— memory chips and other chips (leading from LSI through VLSI to ULSI);

— optical fibre transmission;

— communications satellites;

— optical disk storage using sub-micron technology;

— magnetic storage media;

— laser technology, including laser scanners and laser printers;

— OCR;

— facsimile;

— voice recognition; etc.

This research and development in turn leads to new products and services such as:

— multifunction workstations;

— local area networks (LANs);

— private viewdata systems;

— Euronet-DIANE;

— Prestel (including gateway facilities to other computers);

— value-added networks services (VANS);

— stored program control (SPC) private digital exchanges (PDXs);

— digital transmission services (X-Stream); etc.

The strategy must therefore be prepared by a team whose membership includes someone who is aware of what is happening in the world at large: what is happening in Tokyo, Kawasaki, Osaka and Kyoto – as well as in the USA, France, and West Germany – will affect what is available and what happens in the UK within two or three years. It may not have mattered much before whether UK users kept a close eye on Japanese suppliers but it will matter in the future. Any UK organisation which does not take account of Japanese office systems products is cutting itself off from important office systems developments. For instance, OA strategy planners should be aware of the Toshiba Tosfile Document Filing System, launched in Japan in 1981, and the soon-to-be-announced Integrated Electronic Private Branch Exchange which forms the heart of the NEC integrated electronic office concept. In addition, the strategy team must have someone – perhaps the same person – who can relate technological developments and new products to the organisation, and who can interpret their consequence for the organisation in areas such as:

— the cost of storing information electronically;

— the ease and speed of putting information from non-electronic form into electronic form;

— the ease and speed of searching for and retrieving information.

The convergence of computing and communication will affect office work and gives rise to the concept of the 'creativity office'; this means that OA is perceived as the means of not just raising the productivity of office support personnel but also, and more importantly, of making managers and professionals more creative and raising the quality of the work that they do. Figure 5.11 illustrates the OA Tower of Toshiba. This is a graphical representation of OA as the integration of the three converging technologies of:

— computing ('data processing system');

— office systems ('business machines');

— telecommunications ('communication system').

'Convergence' is shown by the coming together at the apex A of the OA Tower of the three technologies which start from the triangular base of the Tower BCD. Integration is shown in three stages. At the first stage, the lower or first floor of the Tower, we find:

— facsimile machines (integration of office systems with telecommunications);

— OCR machines (integration of office systems with computing).

At the second floor (this is roughly the current position), we find:

— Japanese language word processors;

— electronic document filing system (ie Tosfile);

— electronic telephones;

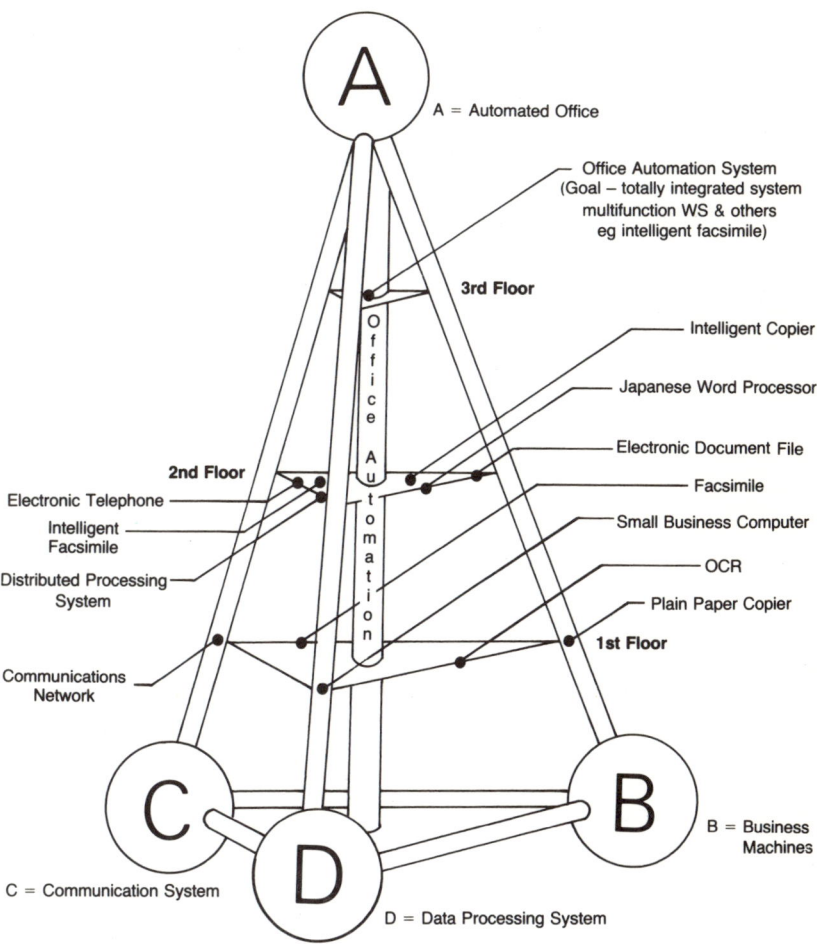

Figure 5.11   The OA Tower of Toshiba

— distributed data processing systems;

— intelligent facsimile machines;

— intelligent copiers.

At the third floor, there will be yet-to-be-announced products and services, eg:

— multifunction workstations connected by local area networks;

— digital SPC PABXs with gateways to external networks;

— teleconferencing;

— value-added network services; etc.

Figure 5.12 illustrates the current state of integration. The inner circles represent office work in a non-automated office; the outer circle shows how these activities can be automated through the use of currently-available solutions. The communication of information can be improved by:

— electronic telephones;

— facsimile;

— computers (including desk top computers);

— plain paper copiers;

— communicating word processors.

The creating and editing of information can be improved by:

— data entry systems;

— word processors;

— computers (including desk top computers);

— plain paper copiers;

— OCR and OMR readers.

The retrieving and editing of information can be improved by:

— word processors;

— computers (including desk top computers);

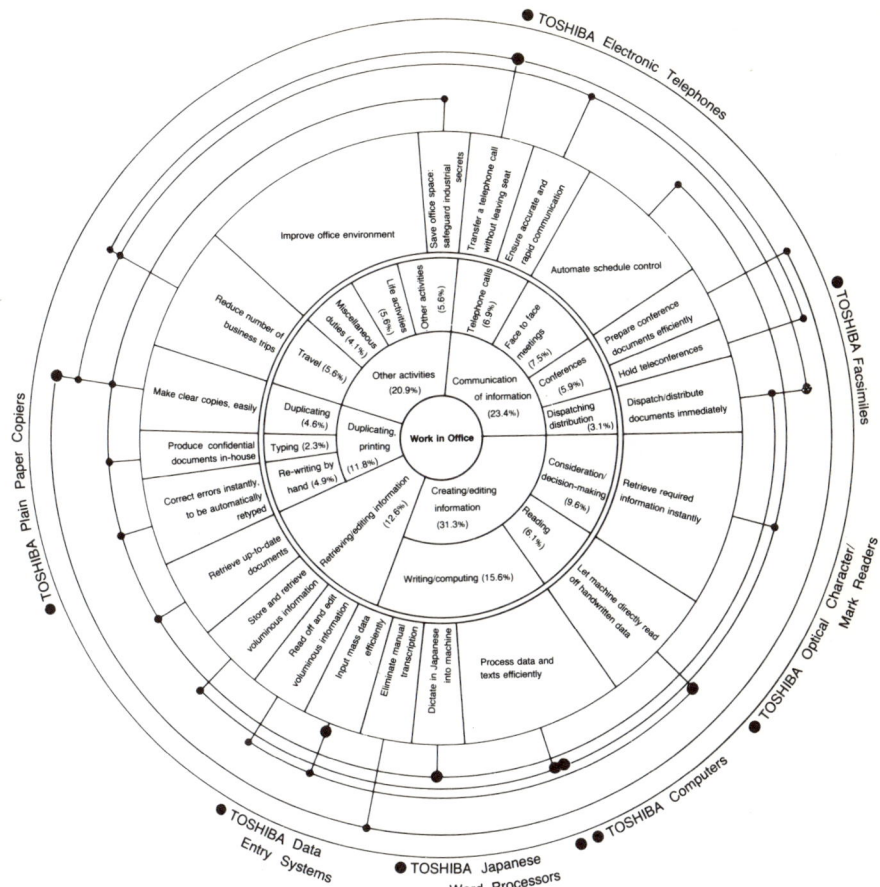

Figure 5.12   Use of Toshiba Products in Office Automation

— OCR and OMR readers;

— data entry systems.

Duplicating and printing can be improved by:

— plain paper copiers;

— facsimile machines;

— word processors.

Travel can be reduced through the use of:

— electronic telephones;

— facsimile machines.

JUSTIFICATION

Justification is a key issue for an OA strategy. The OA planners must identify what it is that the organisation wants the electronic information management systems – and other OA systems which it plans to introduce – to do for them. Note the choice of words: 'what it wants the IMS to do FOR THEM', rather than: 'what each IMS shall do'.

What an IMS does is also important, for this has design implications, but at a strategic level an organisation must ask itself questions such as:

— what information management problems are we encountering currently?

— how will IMS based on curent technology, and new IMS likely to follow from technological developments, help to solve or avoid existing problems, and how will they allow us to raise the quality of our work and productivity?

— what short-term improvements should we seek?

— what mid-term improvements should we seek?

— what long-term improvements should we seek?

The short-term planning horizon may be up to three years ahead. Currently-available IMS may be introduced at once to bring actual benefits. In a large organisation several pilot experiments may be undertaken simultaneously to:

— gain hands-on experience;

— compare how suitable different types of IMS are for the organisation;

— evaluate different types of workstation, different types of user-system interface and different suppliers' approaches to integration;

— investigate the impact of OA upon the organisation.

A smaller organisation may not be able to afford to experiment in this way and may have to regard each small step forward as a way of confirming in practice that the planners' expected benefits can be achieved.

The mid-term planning horizon may be up to seven years ahead. Reasons for deferring the introduction of systems include:

— the organisation does not want to be a 'guinea pig' for a relatively new, untried and untested system;

— a currently-available system is too expensive to justify now, but can be justified later when it is less expensive, has been enhanced, can be piggy-backed or can be integrated with other systems;

— the communications infrastructure must first be enhanced;

— organisational changes (eg centralised filing and administrative support centres) must first be introduced;

— waiting for multifunction workstations;

— waiting for optical disk document filing systems;

— waiting for the outcome of short-term experiments to be completed and evaluated;

— waiting for the organisation's cash flow position to improve.

We must advise organisations against taking a too-cautious approach though, on the basis that the cost in competitive terms of falling behind one's rivals may outweigh the additional short-term expenditure. Organisations should think carefully before deferring the implementation of the OA strategy for too long.

The long-term planning horizon is about ten years ahead. It is not practical to plan this far ahead in detail, but the organisation should have someone who is aware of:

— British Telecom's long-term strategy;

— the content and progress of JIPDEC's fifth generation computer system (FGCS) project in Japan;

— the plans of IBM and AT&T following the settlement of the anti-trust cases in 1981;

— the implications for the organisation due to the availability of:

- voice recognition input (user-dependent and user-independent);

- inference machines;

- virtually unlimited capacity for on-line storage of internal information;

- virtually zero-cost storage for internal information;

- on-line access to all external databases with fast response electronic document delivery systems;

- teleconferencing.

Justification is the process of first identifying, for different types of IMS:

- the expected user advantages;

- any user disadvantages;

- the costs to be incurred;

- the anticipated savings;

- the impact on cash flows;

- the impact on profitability;

- the impact on productivity;

- the impact on employee morale;

- the impact on the organisation's competitiveness;

- the impact on the organisation's relations with customers and suppliers;

- the implications for the organisation's communications infrastructure.

Then it involves assessing whether the value of benefits and savings justifies the costs incurred, and any disadvantages and disruption. As much quantitative information as can be obtained must be brought into the justification decision process – which may be very difficult. There are various constraining factors (see Figure 5.13):

- the very rapid development of technology and consequently the

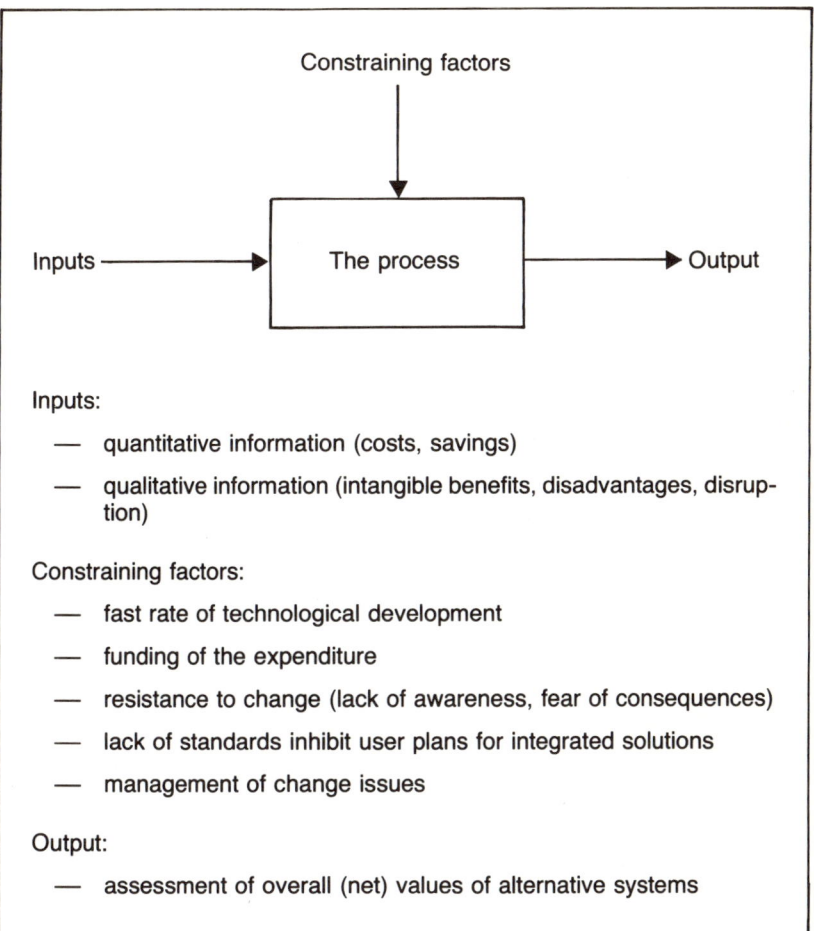

Inputs:

— quantitative information (costs, savings)

— qualitative information (intangible benefits, disadvantages, disruption)

Constraining factors:

— fast rate of technological development

— funding of the expenditure

— resistance to change (lack of awareness, fear of consequences)

— lack of standards inhibit user plans for integrated solutions

— management of change issues

Output:

— assessment of overall (net) values of alternative systems

Figure 5.13   The Justification Process

fast-changing market place, in which new and enhanced products keep appearing and making many existing products obsolete before their pay-back period has been reached and in which new suppliers appear and existing suppliers go out of business;

— an organisation may feel that it cannot afford the short-term expenditure to obtain the long-term benefits; the current recession is affecting many markets, making it difficult for organisations to meet their annual sales targets and to generate the revenue needed for investment; and there are also high interest charges on borrowed money. On the other hand, a company may feel that it cannot afford not to invest in new office technology because that decision leads firstly to its products being uncompetitive in price, secondly to its products being inadequate in terms of quality and performance, and thirdly to the collapse of the company;

— resistance by some employees because of a lack of awareness of the inevitability of the changes which new technology will bring in offices, factories, homes, schools and society generally, and of the importance of making the most of the opportunities to improve the quality of life at work and at leisure; and because of fear of the consequences of change upon their job (ie will it disappear, or become deskilled and boring?), their status and career developments prospects; (NB the employees of an organisation are its most important asset; the user of an office system is the most important aspect of the system: if the user does not use the facilities of a supplied workstation then all the planning, design work and expenditure will have been in vain);

— lack of standards for office systems: eg local area networks, information retrieval command languages, open systems interconnection, viewdata, keyboard design, etc are important areas where progress is slowly being made towards subinternational standards and towards international standards; this lack of standards makes it unnecessarily difficult and expensive for users to plan for the integration of office systems and equipment;

— lack of agreement with the relevant trade unions about the management-of-change issues, such as redeployment, retraining, job evaluation, etc.

Judgements involving an appreciation of the value of intangible and unquantifiable benefits will have to be used in the justification process in determining the relative net values to the organisation of alternative systems. Investment attitudes should not place too much emphasis upon increased productivity, cost savings and quantifiable benefits. These attitudes are probably correct for investment upon machines in factories and for word processors to raise the productivity and throughput of keyboarding specialists.

Office products are now becoming available which are aimed at the manager, the professional, the knowledge worker, and the salesman. These people can and must be made more productive by releasing them from non-productive travel, movement within buildings, queuing, photocopying and other hard-copy document-handling activity, telephone tag, etc, and helping them to put this time to profitable use (eg reading, thinking, writing, communicating). But more important than increased productivity is the need to improve the quality of these people's work, so that:

— the organisation's outputs are better than those of rivals;

— better decisions are taken based on better-quality information;

— the organisation can respond more effectively to events.

One issue which must be confronted concerns the apportionment of investment costs between the organisation as a corporate body and its individual operating units and departments. For if the OA strategy requires investment which cannot be cost-justified in the short term by some user departments, a decision at board level may be necessary to ensure that the strategy can be implemented and long-term benefits achieved.

For further information about benefits and justification, the reader is referred to the NCC publication *Office Technology Benefits* (see Bibliography, item 1.11) which identifies and discusses ten types of benefit which should be considered in the justification process:

— piggybacking;

— a faster flow of information;

— easier access to more information;

— the elimination of paper;

— displaceable costs;

— opportunity hours;

— productivity;

— fewer interruptions;

— better control;

— pilot studies.

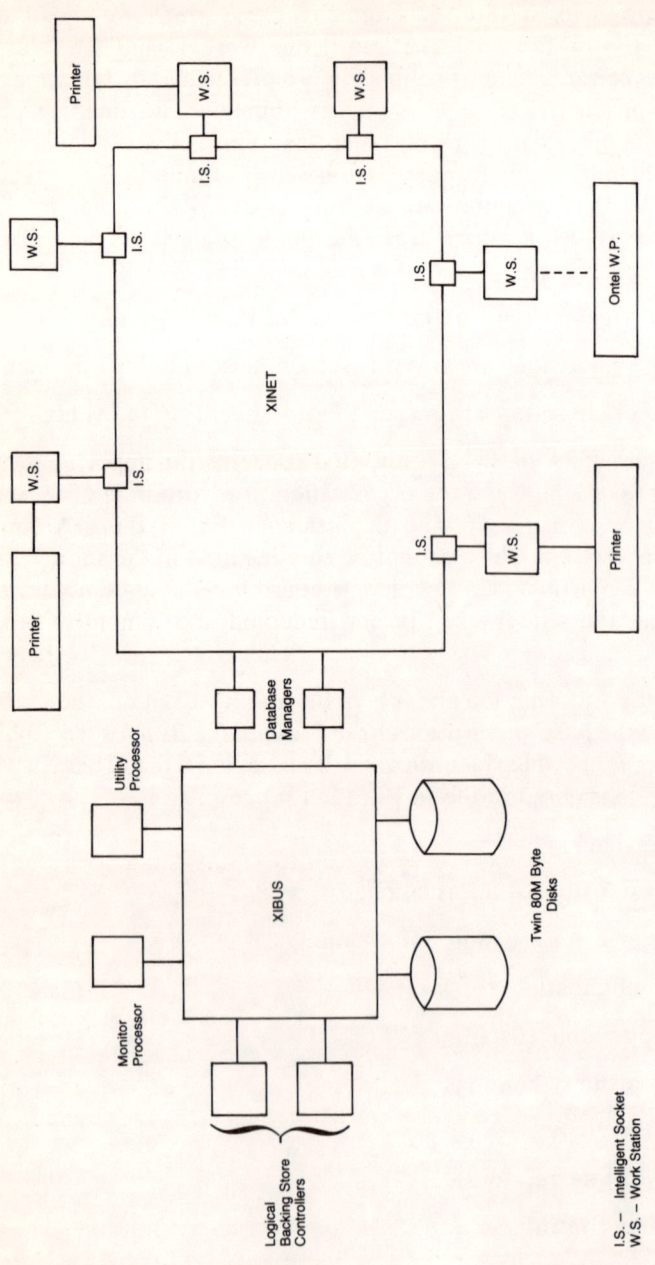

Figure 5.14 LAN Configuration at Scottish Gas – 1981

I.S. – Intelligent Socket
W.S. – Work Station

COMMUNICATIONS INFRASTRUCTURE

The communications infrastucture to support the information flows within a site and across a site's boundary with external networks and services is a key strategic issue. Major developments in this area over the next few years will complicate the strategic planning process by widening the types of communications infrastructure which can be used, but will also benefit the user by providing infrastructures more closely tailored to requirements. The developments arise because of:

— the British Telecommunications Act of 1981 and the enabling powers for the relaxation of British Telecom's monopoly position;

— technological progress and the emergence of new communications products.

The full impact of BT's X-Stream digital transmission services upon OA strategic planning has not yet been felt, but they will have a major impact, as will System X telephone exchanges, communications satellites, the teletex service, the integrated services digital network (ISDN), and other existing and yet-to-be-announced BT services and products. The 1981 Act will gradually extend users' freedom to attach non-BT supplied PABXs and the new generation of intelligent private digital exchanges to the BT network and this will have a major impact on thinking within organisations about what communications infrastructure they need.

At present, there are some organisations which have a PABX, which is the interface between its internal telephone extensions and BT's external PSTN, and which also have a quite separate local area network with separate cabling which interconnects office workstations for internal information flows and maybe an interface between the LAN's controller and the mainframe computer for access to the mainframe and the corporate database. Figure 5.14 illustrates the initial configuration for the Xionics Xinet ring LAN installed in January 1981 at Scottish Gas; Figure 5.15 illustrates how remote Xibus systems could be linked together in a multisite organisation; (NB the ring network to which workstations, word processors, printers, etc, can be attached is called Xinet, and the controller which handles ring control and data management is called a Xibus.)

The majority of information flows in most organisations originate and terminate in the same building and it is entirely sensible for an organisation to install a LAN which initially cannot handle information flows into and out of the site as long as the capability for enhancement in this way is

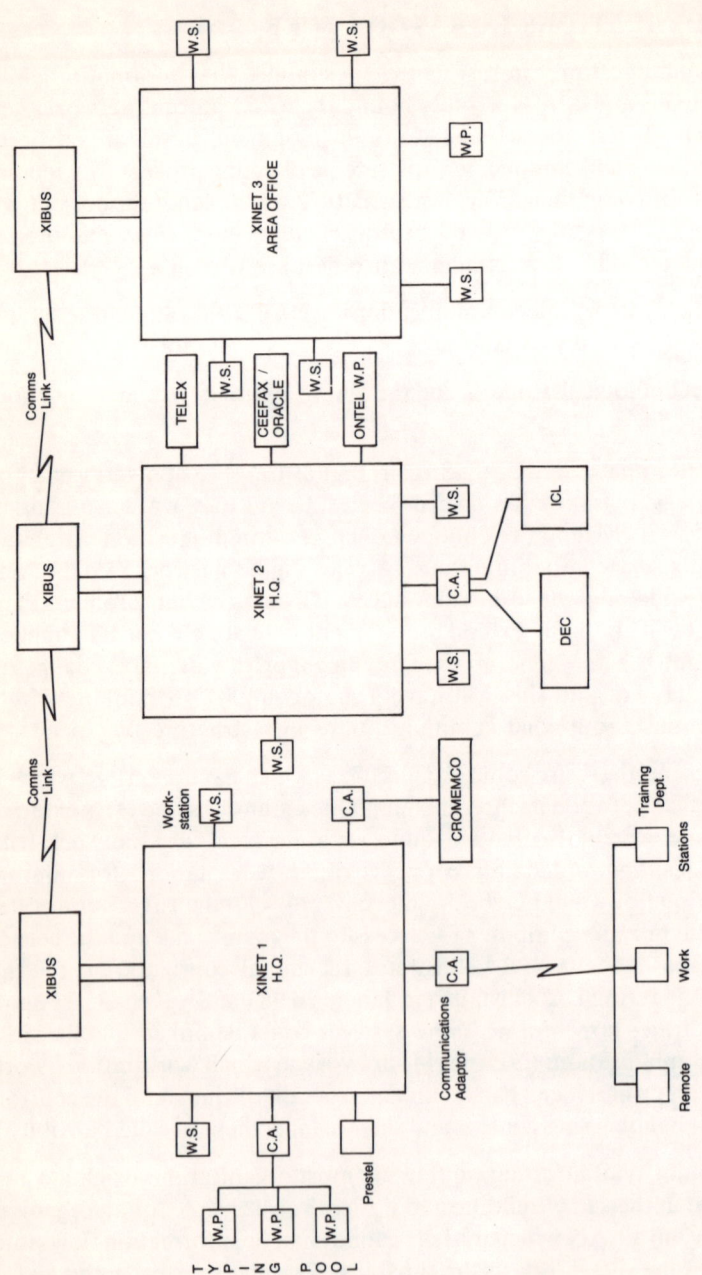

Figure 5.15 Potential LAN Enhancement – Scottish Gas

possible later. A different philosophy is to replace the PABX by an intelligent digital device which forms the bridge between anything and everything and provides overall control. It will be possible to integrate voice conversations with data, text or image information flows simultaneously, using the same existing internal telephone wiring; voice traffic at 64 Kbit/s could be interleaved with data traffic at 56 Kbit/s (with 8 Kbit/s of the capacity of a 128 Kbit/s wire used for traffic control).

At present BT hold the monopoly for the supply of PABXs under 100 extension lines and supplies three stored program control (SPC) electronic switchboards ('call connect' systems): Herald, Monarch and Regent. Above 100 extension lines, there are a few manufactures whose exchanges have been approved including:

— ITT 4080 (analogue switching);

— IBM 3750 and 1750 (both analogue switching);

— Plessey PDX 800, (marked by Plessey and Telephone Rentals) (digital switching);

— GEC SL1 VLE (digital switching);

— Philips EBX 8000 (reed relay switching).

The British Telecommunications Act of 1981 removed BTs monopoly on the supply of equipment for connection to the public telephone network, but its measures do not become fully effective until July 1983, three years after Sir Keith Joseph's initial announcement that the monopoly was to be lifted.

The three-year period was a part of deliberate phasing-in period to give British industry time to put products on the market to *compete with imports* from the USA and elsewhere. It also gave time to draw up the necessary *technical standards* to which equipment connected to BT's networks must conform.

The Act itself is not specific in terms of what is and what is not permitted. It is a piece of enabling legislation placing the real power in the hands of the Secretary of State for Industry. As far as PABXs are concerned, the situation is as follows:

— the British Standards Institution (BSI) is drawing up a standard for PABXs, to be published in July 1983. Once the standard is published, any supplier will be able to submit a PABX to the British

Approval Board for Telecommunications (BABT, part of the British Electro-technical Approvals Board (BEAB) and independent of BT) for evaluation against this standard. Only models which conform to the standard will be permitted connection to the BT network;

— until the PABX standard is published and PABXs are 'liberalised' the existing situation prevails: BT have a monopoly on the supply, installation and maintenance of PABXs less than 100 lines, and on the associated extension telephones and wiring ('block wiring'); above 100 extensions BT have approved certain PABXs for private supply and installation, but retain their monopoly on the supply and installation of extension telephones and wiring, and on maintenance of the whole system;

— after July 1983, all PABXs together with extension instruments and wiring will be open to competitive supply and installation. BT will continue to do the commissioning and acceptance testing of all PABXs, and to approve the wiring;

— non-BT maintenance will be permitted on time division SPC PABXs installed after July 1983. Other types of PABX and ALL PABXs installed before July 1983 will continue to be maintained by BT as at present;

— to improve the choice of large PABXs available to users before July 1983, *six* PABXs (including Thorn Ericsson MD110, Mitel SX 2000, Ferranti-GTE GTD 1000 and GTD 4000, Harris D 1200) have been selected by the Department of Industry in consultation with BT, to undergo an accelerated BT approval procedure. This move was announced in January 1982 and approval is expected to take about a year.

A new generation of intelligent digital machines, operating under stored program control (SPC), may then become available and approved for attachment to the PSTN. Datapoint has announced its ISX (Information Switching Exchange) in the USA; Nippon Electric Corporation may soon announce its Intelligent Electronic Private Branch Exchange; and Plessey has announced that its PDX (Private Digital Exchange) will form the heart of its Integrated Business Information System (IBIS) strategy for the electronic office – IBIS was launched in June 1982 and exhibited at two London exhibitions, Business Efficiency Exhibition (at Earls

Court) and Office Automation Show (at Barbican Centre). Northern Telecom, Wang, IBM, Rolm, Fujitsu and other manufacturers can be expected to launch products in what may prove to be an expanding and lucrative market worldwide. A generic term of this type of machine has not yet emerged but the following are some of the terms that have been suggested:

— private digital exchange;

— computerised branch exchange;

— office controller;

— intelligent switch.

This type of intelligent SPC machine will be more than a third-generation PABX for handling internal and external telephone calls and other information flows using the internal telephone wiring and the PSTN. It will be able to route all conversational and stored voice, text, data and facsimile flows between workstations, computer terminals, word processors, office computers, mainframe and minicomputers, local area network controllers, etc, within a building, and form a gateway to external facilities such as the PSTN and private circuits, telex, teletex, PSS, Prestel, remote mainframes, electronic mail and other public and private services. Its facilities will include:

— communications protocol conversation;

— code conversion;

— speed conversion;

— routeing (ie choice of cheapest alternative if several services can be used, and choice of best time of day to send the information);

— switching;

— store-and-forwarding of messages;

— monitoring of usage for information flows;

— energy consumption and control (ie heating, lighting);

— security control.

Figure 5.16 illustrates how such an office control computer might function at the hub of all voice and non-voice information flows and

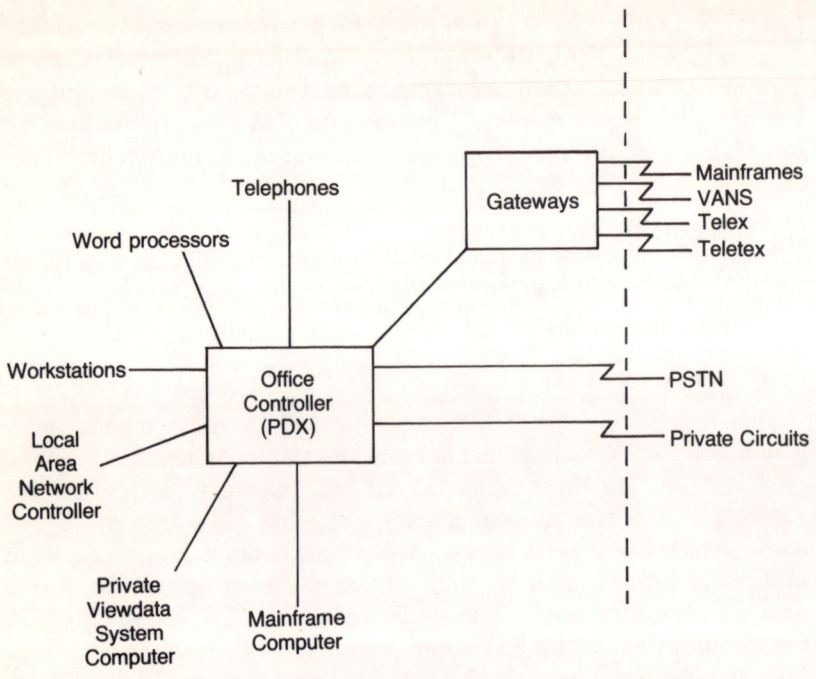

Figure 5.16   Private Digital Exchange Architecture

information processing.

It is sometimes argued that a major advantage of this type of approach is that existing internal telephone wiring can be used, but although this may be so it does seem that an even more significant point in favour of this approach is that it integrates the various information management flows and processes, incompatible hardware and external networks and services. Within a building, there may be a role for coaxial cabling and optical fibre cabling instead of, or in addition to, the existing twisted-pair telephone wiring – time will tell.

A limitation with some existing digital PABXs which handle voice and data/text is that they are designed primarily for voice traffic and the different characteristics of data/text flows can cause a condition called 'blocking'. This means that two idle lines cannot be interconnected because all possible paths between them within the PABX are already in use. The new generation of PDXs should overcome this problem.

A number of selected articles (see Bibliography, items 5.1 to 5.11) about this important and fast-changing area are drawn to the reader's attention; one of these (item 5.8) reviews currently-available LANs.

MANAGEMENT OF CHANGE

Many readers have seen their organisation move from being a non-computer user to being a computer user dependent upon the availability of its computer installation – to perform many financial, commercial and management data processing applications – and upon the integrity of its data files (including back-up copies). We have also seen new computing facilities being brought into use, eg real-time transaction processing systems, on-line enquiries into the corporate database from computer terminals, word processing systems, and terminals linked to external computers. Most readers may therefore have experienced considerable change.

We anticipate considerable changes in offices over the next decade, though many people cannot appreciate the degree and nature of the changes which will occur. Some cannot accept that technological developments which are being forecast can be achieved; others accept that technological developments can occur but are reluctant to change habits and practices under technological pressure. We believe that change will and must occur and that *if managed properly* it will bring enormous benefits throughout society.

In the context of OA, the changes which will occur, and which must be planned for, include:

— reducing the use of paper and eliminating its use wherever possible; information will migrate to electronic media;

— changing from paper-based filing systems to electronic filing systems;

— regrouping secretarial and other support staff into administrative support centres (ASCs), ie larger units supporting several departments;

— giving office workers a workstation and expecting them to be able to think whilst using its facilities; ie the workstation becomes

integrated into their creative thinking and decision-making processes;

— the electronic office will become a system rather than a place;
people will work away from the office (as a place) to a much
greater extent than they do today; paradoxically, perhaps, there
will be more, and more effective, face-to-face meetings between
managers, between managers and those whom they manage, and
between professional colleagues; this is because:

— such meetings will continue to be important;

— office technology will make it easier to arrange meetings at
times when most people can be present;

— office technology will make meetings more effective
because participants can brief themselves better
beforehand, and can use up-to-date information during
meetings;

— redeploying and retraining personnel.

The ability to manage and motivate people will continue to be as
important in the electronic office as it has ever been. During the period of
change within organisations, as office technology is introduced, qualities
of perception, judgement and understanding of people will be crucial.

How can an organisation prepare for and manage change? It has to
learn from the experience of others to avoid making the same mistakes; it
has to capitalise on what seems to be successful. There are many ways in
which organisations can gain experience, distill it and disseminate information and good practices internally. See also Bibliography, items 5.12 to
5.19.

The concept of a user group has been successfully adopted for many
years in data processing, particularly for companies who use a particular
supplier's mainframe computer, or who use a particular software product
from a software house. Representatives from user companies form a user
group and meet regularly to share experiences and act as a pressure group
to co-ordinate requests for enhancements, better documentation, better
user support, etc. NCC extended this concept to computer security when
it launched its Security Awareness Scheme in December 1978; this 'club'
is now thriving with about 160 subscribing members. In the February
1980 issue of *EDP Analyzer* (see Bibliography, item 5.14), there is a

report on the activities and organisation of two office automation 'user roundtables' in the USA. In 1982, NCC launched an Office Technology Circle to provide opportunities for organisations to attend meetings to discuss strategic planning, managment of change, and other OA topics of interest and concern to them; (NB readers may also be interested in the Communications Circle launched at the same time).

Some of the companies we have spoken to have participated as subscribers in multi-client funded studies – such as the Booz, Allen and Hamilton study (see Bibliography, item 5.20) and NCC's Office and Communications Systems Division's own study *Managers and the New Technology* (see Bibliography, item 1.9). Others have participated in research programmes such as those run by The Office Technology Research Group, the Diebold Group, Butler Cox & Partners and Eosys (formerly Urwick Nexos). Other ways of gaining experience and discussing issues include:

— participating in the work of standards-making organisations;

— participating in the activities of specialist groups belonging to professional societies;

— attending meetings, seminars and workshops;

— funding research programmes at universities.

Within an organisation, awareness of OA may diffuse slowly at first, led by a small group of professional innovators. At some point, perhaps as long as two or three years later, those who lead opinion will become interested in OA and perceive its benefits. Then it will become fashionable within the organisation to want to use OA systems and their use will spread quickly. This rationale may resemble more closely than people like to admit how new technology will be introduced into many organisations.

An organisation should not sit back and wait for OA systems to be introduced. It should have a strategy, but it should not direct departments and individuals to change – at least not without consultation. It may be clear from internal consultation that an organisation should set objectives such as 'the elimination of 90% of paper within five years' and it will help to bring this about by gradually withdrawing paper-based information.

An organisation may set up a committee to have overall direction for the OA programme, and a team to prepare the strategy. It should also consider setting up a team to be responsible for the implementation of new systems, and for redeployment and retraining issues. There is conflicting advice about how such participation by employees should be sought by those preparing the OA strategy, but we feel that employee and union attitudes towards new technology are becoming more positive and that management should encourage employee involvement.

We are impressed by aspects of the Japanese style of management, which we discussed with Japanese managers during our visit to Tokyo and also with some of the other organisations we have spoken to. We found strong evidence in several Japanese organisations of:

— trust and co-operation between management, employees and unions;

— employee participation in the decision-making process;

— understanding of and commitment to corporate objectives by all employees;

— a caring attitude towards employees;

— a commitment to quality;

— an absence of cynicism.

It is possible that OA will cause job displacement on a large scale and place the management/worker relationship under stress, but it does appear that the Japanese culture, attitudes to change and industrial relations will help Japan to cope with the changes associated with OA (see also Bibliography, item 5.18).

Western culture however is different from Japanese; we do not think it possible for UK organisations to adopt Japanese attitudes, even if they wanted to, in time to provide a different environment for the introduction of OA and the management of change. But UK organisations should study Japanese culture and its beneficial impact on factory and office work and try to introduce, gradually over a period of time, changes appropriate to Western culture.

In the UK, new technology agreements between organisations and unions will cover more and more organisations and employees. They will seek to share fairly the benefits of OA, and to avoid undesirable consequences. There will be less focus on increased pay and more focus on such factors as:

— increased leave;

— sabbatical leave;

— shorter hours per week;

— flexible work hours (for shopping, gardening, sport, social work, etc);

— voluntary early retirement;

— retraining programmes;

— reduced travel to work (to reduce stress);

— less interruptions during periods of creative-thinking activity;

— better administrative support;

— ergonomically-designed workstations and offices.

The undesirable consequences which can arise and should be avoided or minimised include:

— compulsory redundancies;

— reduction in the total number of jobs in an organisation;

— deskilling of work;

— boredom;

— loss of face-to-face contact between human beings.

User acceptance will be crucial during the migration to the fully integrated electronic office. Training programmes will make considerable use of audio-visual training material and the user's workstation itself will also feature strongly in these programmes as the user will receive instruction through it from computer-aided learning programmes. Even more important than instructing office workers how to use office systems is the issue of what these systems should be used for.

People must learn to think of information as a resource, and of information management as an activity which adds value which was not there before. This will require very considerable changes of attitude at all levels of employment and society, for many existing practices serve no other purpose than to:

— keep people employed and busy (and therefore prevent them from doing something useful);

—   maintain the organisation's pecking order, the status of some of its
    senior personnel, at the same time discouraging its junior person-
    nel from having to think.

In short, people must begin to THINK INFORMATION. (See also
Bibliography, items 5.22 to 5.24).

Finally a few comments should be made about attitudes of UK trade
unions. Generally we feel that they are more aware of new technology
and positive towards it than is commonly believed to be the case, although
there are variations from one union to another. The APEX union has
produced two excellent reports, one as long ago as March 1979. Another
has been produced by BIFU (see Bibliography, items 5.25 to 5.27). For
some time, the civil service unions have been seeking a new technology
agreement and one, the Society of Civil and Public Servants (SCPS), not
wanting to co-operate over the introduction of office technology unless a
new technology agreement had been reached, was threatening industrial
action if the DoI installed a private viewdata system in advance of an
agreement. In March 1982, it was reported that the Council of Civil
Service Unions had accepted an interim new technology agreement for
two years (see Bibliography, items 5.28 to 5.33).

The following comments were made by trade union officers from BIFU
and APEX who attended NCC workshops in 1981 to discuss IMS
strategic planning (the first two comments are from the BIFU officer, the
others from the APEX officer):

—   one concern is that there should be good, and free, communication
    between management and unions; new technology agreements
    are sought by unions to provide an identifiable framework for
    discussion and to formalise timescales; the new skills for the
    electronic office must be identified and employees must be given
    appropriate training and grading/remuneration for new skills;
    communication blocks arise when management are unwilling to
    provide information which they wish to keep as a commercial
    secret, for the time being, because they do not want competitors to
    know what they are planning to do, but both management and
    unions must establish a mutual trust to prevent unnecessary con-
    frontation;

—   another concern is the impact of new technology upon employ-
    ment . . . management and unions should recognise and accept

their social responsibility to provide as much work as they can and to share work out as equitably as they can . . . ;

— my union . . . is concerned over the effect . . . of new technology upon the availability of jobs, but feels that a Luddite attitude . . . will lead to companies not surviving. So my union accepts new technology – but not at any price;

— there is concern that companies do not train staff adequately to use new office machines; often, because of lack of consultation with users, equipment is not use and gathers dust in a corner;

— there is concern that secretaries should not have their jobs changed in such a way that they become like those in a production line at a factory; jobs must consist of a variety of tasks, and must enable initiative to be used;

— there is concern that ergonomic issues should be properly dealt with in the design of screen-based systems;

— unions like to be brought into talks about *system design* much earlier than is the case at present (NB there does not seem to be any conflict here with the view frequently expressed by management that unions should not be brought too early into *strategic planning* talks, for otherwise it will be difficult ever to converge upon a corporate policy for OA);

— unions desire to have a greater degree of consultation;

— it is very important that management should plan and prepare for the changes that will accompany new technology;

— the benefits of new technology should be shared (eg shorter working hours, more leave, a sabbatical leave of absence).

6 Design Considerations

SUITABILITY FOR TASK (ie TASK FIT)

Information management systems in the electronic office should seek to meet the needs of their users, to help them to perform more effectively the work which they are employed and paid to do by providing them quickly and conveniently with accurate, up to date and relevant information in order to:

— improve the quality of decision-making, reports and other output;

— to increase turnover;

— to make the organisation better able to respond to its customers and to situations.

It is too easy to take the negative and unimaginative view that OA is primarily or simply about:

— automating existing tasks;

— cutting costs;

— doing things more quickly ('time compression');

— raising the productivity of office workers;

— creating opportunity-hours.

Each of these issues must be taken into consideration in deciding what types of IMS are needed and justified, and what are the functional requirements of workstations for different categories of office worker. However the main thrust must come from a realisation (and this may need quite a degree of change of perception!) that information is an important resource and that OA must be used to manage this resource more effectively to add more value to office activities.

Let us consider next the following questions:

— why do people need information (ie the purpose);

— what information do people need (ie the type);

— how can people obtain information (ie the channel);

· — where can people obtain information from (ie the source)?

Office workers need information in order to:

— keep well informed and up to date about the organisation's administration and operations;

— keep well informed and up to date about competitors;

— keep well informed and up to date about external developments relevant to their work;

— prepare lectures and reports;

— take decisions; etc.

Office workers need information about:

— organisation structures, budgets, products, sales and other performance statistics relating to the organisation;

— products and sales statistics relating to competitors;

— market research, research and development in relevant areas, legislation, etc.

IMS do not change the reasons why office workers need information nor the type of information which they need to receive. On the other hand, IMS do affect the ways in which people can obtain information and the sources from which they can seek it, and therefore those organisations who are in the business of providing information must move with the times, be responsive to users, and provide information in electronic form instead of, or as well as, in non-electronic form, and /or provide users with electronic means for searching for abstracted or indexed information.

Conventionally, people obtain information from:

— personal, departmental and corporate paper-based filing systems;

— public libraries, private libraries or the organisation's reference library;

— personal contact with other people (through face-to-face meetings, telephone calls, telex messages, letters, etc).

In future, there will be a significant shift towards obtaining information in electronic form, or using computer-based information retrieval systems to locate relevant paper-based information. People will then obtain information (several organisations, of course, already do) through the following channels:

— Prestel;

— private viewdata systems on an in-house computer;

— private viewdata systems on a viewdata computer bureau (eg via Prestel Gateway or a private gateway);

— access to the corporate database on the mainframe computer;

— access to shared personal and departmental files via a fileserver unit attached to a local area network;

— Euronet-DIANE, Lockheed Dialog or other external public on-line databases.

At present people obtain information from paper-based (and similar) sources such as:

— books;

— reports;

— journals;

— manuals;

— letters;

— microfilm/microfiche;

— slides/transparencies;

— films;

— radio and TV programmes (live and recorded);

— audio-visual cassettes; etc.

In future, there will be a shift towards using computers from a desk-top workstation to bring to the office worker:

— information which he requires and which is held in electronic form, (eg a viewdata frame, records from the corporate database);

— electronic references to information which he requires and which is held in paper form (or similar).

The purpose of obtaining information and the type of information required depends on the occupation of the worker (eg manager, corporate planner, designer, lecturer, salesman, research worker) and what task is being undertaken (eg preparing a plan, writing an article, preparing a lecture, updating a file, etc).

The channels used to search for and retrieve information depend upon their accessibility, ease of use, cost of usage and effectiveness. The sources of information are selected for their availability and the quality of their contents. Of course the quality of the content of an information source should be one of the most important criteria, perhaps the most important, in deciding what information to retrieve. Nevertheless, many people prefer easily-available information to better-quality information which is difficult to obtain. Stored information should be structured in a way appropriate for the task for which it is intended to be used; a user should not have to spend too much time in interpreting or formatting retrieved information.

Indeed in every organisation probably, and to a much greater degree than people are prepared to admit, there is good-quality information which is being wasted because colleagues do not know of its existence or cannot cope with the hassle of acquiring it from paper-based filing systems, as well as the problem of colleagues unknown to each other duplicating each other's work of obtaining the same information from the same, or different, sources. IMS will provide opportunities for colleagues to be more open with each other and to share the results of their information searches and managers must motivate those whom they manage to co-operate in this way, if they are not used to doing so. It would be worthwhile through questionnaires and brainstorming sessions for IMS systems designers to find out what their colleagues' information needs really are, and how these can best be met in the electronic office.

EASE OF USE

For many years now, many office workers have been 'users' of mainframe data processing applications programs and this has taken away some of the tedious error-prone drudgery of performing hundreds or thousands of numerical computations, of sorting records alphabetically or by date of birth or by some other parameter, of merging two sets of records (eg existing records on file and updates), or (simply using the computer as a fast printer) of writing or photocopying. These users may have used the computer in batch processing mode in which case they may have learned to organise their work so as to take account of the fact that output will not be available for several hours after, or until the day following, input. For the most part they will be largely unaware of and unaffected by any of the frequent occurrences of short-duration system unavailability due to planned preventive maintenance, system dumping, system enhancement, operator error, computer, disk drive or printer malfunction, or whatever. Many office workers however have experience of using on-line systems where from a VDU they can update records in files, interrogate files in the corporate database or applications program files, or perform transaction processing, whilst many programmers have experience of on-line program development. These people will know of the intense frustration caused by even short periods of system unavailability because of their impact upon short-term deadlines or upon services being rendered to customers of the organisation. However, most on-line systems are now designed to be very reliable, to give users a fast response time and to give users helpful information during any periods of system degradation or downtime.

Office automation systems for the electronic office require to be easy to use – this is of paramount importance. Several people say that this is the most important aspect of all for system designers. Only functionality and reliability, perhaps, merit more attention. Reliability is important because the OA system user has to make a total commitment to the system if the full benefits of new technology are to be attained; a half-hearted approach is a waste of the investment in the system and of the user's training, and is unfair to colleagues. However friendly the user-system interface has been designed to be, users will not make that commitment if the system is unreliable. A user of an unreliable electronic filing system will feel as frustrated as would someone who is locked out of his office or who has lost the key to his filing cabinet. Functionality is important because an OA system is not very useful if it does only some of the things users want, however easy it may be to use the system and even if it is available whenever the user wishes to use it. We believe that functionality, reliability and ease-of-use are all very important, that there is no

need for manufacturers to give one of these design issues less consideration that the others. It is now possible for suppliers to discover from field
trials or from independent in-depth reports by UK and USA consultancy
firms and others not only what functions are important but also what
constitutes an easy to use OA system. Progress in chip technology makes
it possible for a multifunction, reliable and user-friendly workstation to
be a reality.

There are three aspects of user friendliness:

— an ergonomically-designed workstation;

— an ergonomically-designed working environment;

— an easy-to-learn, easy-to-remember and easy-to-use high-level
  user dialogue; eg a high-level command language or a menu
  selection procedure.

Some of the workstations available in the UK towards the end of 1981
and early in 1982 were quite well designed and reasonably user-friendly,
but not yet cheap enough for most users to be able to justify or to afford
(this is not quite the same thing, as local authorities constrained by cash
limits and private sector companies constrained by high interest rates on
borrowed money will know) putting one on the desk of each office
worker. Pressure from users and market competitive forces have made
suppliers pay attention to the needs of users. Unfortunately the same
cannot be said of user organisations in the UK. Management remain
largely unaware that an ergonomically-designed working environment is
an important design issue for office systems and that they are responsible
for low productivity that accompanies a badly-designed office. APEX,
BIFU and some other trades unions with members employed in offices
have done important work in this area (see Bibliography, items 5.25, 5.26
and 5.27). It is likely that from now on trades unions in the office sector
will pay much more attention to an ergonomically-designed working
environment in the office and will provide the thrust which will cause
management to respond.

One method of accessing information is viewdata. Certain public
information is held on Prestel, on which closed user groups can be formed
for corporate information. Organisations can install in-house private
viewdata systems or use a viewdata bureau service. On the other hand
information can be stored in databases and retrieved by information
retrieval packages. Generally, viewdata users flip through a tree structure

of index pages selecting options from each menu in turn to progress further towards the relevant information frames. Viewdata databases cannot always be searched using keywords (although this is possible with the Japanese Captain system), or combinations of codes or headings, as is the case with information retrieval packages. Here users have to learn and remember the command language of an information retrieval package and can be confused, because of the lack of standardisation, if several command languages are used to access different databases. Viewdata systems are not always easy to use, for users can sometimes get lost, as in a maze, because:

— the structure is often 'fuzzy';

— labels are ambiguous and inconsistent;

— it is difficult to backtrack successfully because of system and human memory limitations.

On-line information retrieval systems are still too difficult for many users to use because of:

— the variety of host computers and different access command languages in use;

— the variety of network procedures;

— the variety of terminals, keyboard functions and layout, and local filing procedures; etc.

This problem has been taken up by the CEC which has launched a study to solve some of the difficulties of this type experienced by users of Euronet-DIANE. Specific problems which this study could address include:

— automatic transfer of search questions from one host to another;

— simplifying access to host computers to suit the skill levels of individual users;

— automatic conversion of the access command language jargon to normal every-day language;

— multilingual aids to translate key terms or text.

It is too early to predict what the outcome of this study will be, whether it will lead to some kind of adaptor fitted to users' terminals, or a 'black-box' attached to hosts' computers, or something else.

Ease-of-use depends upon:

— operations and procedures which the users find logical;

— appropriate system response times;

— adequate feedback to the user;

— error controls (prevention, detection and correction);

— system flexibility and adaptability;

— consistency and compatibility at all system levels;

— appropriate user/system dialogue; (NB different users have differing needs, for example experienced and naive users may require
   different prompts and the former may use abbreviated commands);

— appropriate screen formatting and information coding.

The most important design consideration for an electronic office system, as for an interactive on-line computer system, is the aptness of the
system for its users. Two NCC publications with the same title, *Designing
Systems for People,* one a book and the other a guidelines document, give
helpful information (see Bibliography, items 6.1 and 6.2).

USE OF EXISTING NETWORKS

At the Amoco Production Company Research Centre in Tulsa, it was
decided not to use existing telephone wires when 575 terminals were
installed, although this approach would have avoided a major rewiring
problem, because terminal response times would have been unacceptably
long; instead coaxial cables were put in. These cables had a much faster
data transfer rate of about 10 Mbit/s and, of course, no modems were
required.

USER LANGUAGE FACILITIES

One of the problems of user-unfriendliness facing the majority of office
workers who wish to access on-line databases is the complexity of the
command language to access, search and perform other functions in
relation to the database, or more accurately the difficulty of remembering
the details of the command language which the user needs to use at any

particular moment. For example does one key in

    SHOW   R=1

or SHOW   R1

to display the contents of the first record found in a search, or does one use the command

    FIND

or SEARCH

or SEEK

to find words in a database.

Most existing command languages have either been supplied by mainframe manufacturers to give their computers a competitive edge (eg STATUS for ICL and STAIRS for IBM), or developed by the computer staff of the database host organisation to give their service a competitive edge over rival on-line information retrieval services.

In the case of Euronet-DIANE, the CEC sponsored a project to develop a Common Command Language (CCL) to overcome the problems of lack of standards in respect of the use of bibliographic databases. Figure 6.1 illustrates the problem and the progress (at September 1981). Several Euronet-DIANE host services have promised to offer CCL and it is already available on the European Space Agency's IRS service in Frascati, Italy and some others.

SECURITY

NCC has produced many books and reports on the subject of computer security since the formation in 1975 of the Centre's Computer Security and Privacy Division, (see Bibliography, item 6.3). There is now an on-going club for organisations interested in this subject, launched in December 1978 as the Security Awareness Scheme and revised and renamed in 1982 as the Security Circle.

Computer security is concerned with the identification of accidental and deliberate threats whose occurrence can cause a loss of computer system availability, integrity or confidentiality and with the preparation and implementation of a computer security programme of countermeasures which gives an adequate and cost-effective level of protection. It is,

Command Languages([1])	Hosts which use them	CCL
STAIRS ([2]) (IBM)	– CNUCE, CITERE, IAEA, HOECHST DATACENTRALEN, SPIDEL	Planned for CNUCE, others investigating.
	– BELINDIS, DATASTAR, G.CAM	Not planned
GRIPS/DIRS 3 (Siemens)	– DIMDI, ECHO, FIZ-TECHNIK, GID, INKA	Available
MISTRAL (CII-HB)	– TELESYSTEMES-QUESTEL, EURIS, BNDO	Planned for Questel
STATUS (ICL)	– FINSBURY	Not planned
QUEST/RECON (derived from Lockheed's DIALOG)	– ESA – IRS	Available
ELHILL (derived from SDC's ORBIT)	– BLAISE	Not planned
FIND (home-bred)	– CED	Planned
UNIDAS (home-bred)	– CILEA	Available

[1] Refers only to hosts with bibliographic reference databases. CCL does not cover databanks.
[2] Various versions of STAIRS in use.

Figure 6.1   Euronet-DIANE Common Command Language (CCL)

of course, also concerned with contingency planning to handle, if this becomes necessary, stand-by operation and the recovery to normal operation, and with security auditing of the computer security programme and of the contingency plan.

Do office systems raise any new security issues, which require a different approach to that followed in the security of mainframe-based DP systems with on-line terminal access? Basically the security issues are just the same, but some points can be highlighted. In the electronic office, users will come to commit themselves to their workstation and the availability at all times of the facilities and services which it provides as a stand-alone microcomputer or word processor or as a multifunction device with communications links to other workstations, to computers and to value-added network services. Availability is of crucial importance for two reasons:

— periods of non-availability will disrupt the office worker, interrupting the flow of thinking, writing, communicating, etc; there will be frustration as in a conventional paper-based office when disruptions occur and, for whatever reason, the filing cabinets cannot be used;

— recurring periods of non-availability will cause office workers to be apathetic about electronic office systems, or, having committed themselves once, lead to them reverting to paper; this would be very bad because:

  — paper-based methods of office work are inefficient and ineffective as compared to electronic methods;

  — users will be faced with the inconvenience of operating a dual system of paper and electronic methods;

  — there will be a danger of losing the 'critical mass' of users, which is so important if the full OA benefits are to be attained.

Several users have commented to us on the acceptable level of reliability of their new OA systems, but one disgruntled manager with responsibility for introducing a pilot OA system during 1980/81 into the Management Services Division of a UK company had a different story to tell. This is summarised below because user organisations need to know what the pitfalls can be:

— 'We installed a local area network late in 1980 with nine workstations located in Management Services Division (MSD). We believed that the hands-on experience would be beneficial to help MSD to:

  — define the enhancements we would want to ask the supplier to provide later;

  — prepare a case for the justification of the extension of the system into user departments;

  — plan for the implementation of the system in user departments.

A year later enthusiasm has given way to frustration. A decision had been taken to move to a new building and it was hoped that a decision could also be made – following a successful one-year pilot OA experiment

– to enhance the local area network system and to introduce it into user departments. But the experiment has not been a success because of the local area network's unacceptably low reliability, despite the system being acceptable from the ease-of-use and functionality points of view. The reliability has been so bad that several of the users during the experiment have not been able to form a view of whether they find the system useful or not, because they have not used it enough. Typically, they would switch the workstation on and see displayed a message informing them that they could not use the system until further notice because of a fault. The faults have been reported to the supplier, but there are contractual problems about who is responsible for paying for any replacement of electronic equipment that may be agreed to be necessary.'

So this manager was fighting a defensive rearguard action with his board at a time when he hoped to be implementing the second phase. His problems were compounded by:

— the recession during 1980/81;

— malicious bomb alarm telephone calls which, because of the internal wiring, led to the electricity supply to the local network being cut off and recent work being lost;

— on average 10 out of 50 electronic point-of-sale terminals at outlets for the company's products in the UK being inoperative every day!

Users of most computer systems are unaware of the security dumping that has to be carried out. This activity has to be performed for office systems too, but must be done outside normal office hours and if possible at a time when users are not wanting to use the system (ie the needs of managers, professionals, sales force personnel, etc, who work late to meet deadlines, or who dial in from home or hotel rooms must be taken into account in scheduling security dumping). It might be appropriate to design an office system so that users could access and read, but not alter files, during periods of security dumping.

There have been some major strikes by computer operators in the UK, particularly in the public sector, eg at selected civil service computer installations, telephone billing computer centres. This has caused some managements to look to distributed computing and some user departments to look to stand-alone microcomputers as a way of minimising the disruption caused by such strikes. It may be one reason why some users wish to have a self-contained office system, rather than terminals to a mainframe. Of course some of the work performed at a workstation requires access to the mainframe computer and to the corporate database and some does not. The controller (the computer which controls or co-ordinates the operation of the local network) is often placed in the computer room, along with the shared printer, the shared fileserver and other shared resources. However it is not such a problem to operate these facilities if the operators go on strike as it is to operate a mainframe computer, but if office staff are reluctant to cross picket lines it may be appropriate to place the controller in the office area.

Office systems provide workstations at the place of work of each and every person, so the security measure of restricting terminals to high security terminal rooms is not appropriate. The use of workstations must be controlled by passwords and access control software; in the last three or four years there have been great improvements in access control software for mainframes and these same techniques must be provided for office systems to prevent fraud, tampering with files, unauthorised use of resources, etc (see Bibliography, item 6.4).

Much concern is continuing to be expressed in the UK that the UK has no privacy legislation for computer systems and that this is taking us further out of line with other countries with whom our laws should be in harmony. Privacy legislation in the UK may be enacted in Parliament, though, at any time (see Bibliography, item 6.5). NCC has had a strong interest in this subject for over a decade and has completed joint studies with Gesellschaft fur Mathematik und Datenverarbeitung (GMD) (in Germany) and INRIA (in France). In particular, it has produced a draft code of practice for word processing (see Bibliography, item 6.6). In April 1982, the UK government published a privacy White Paper (see Bibliography, item 6.7) and in the Queen's Speech (November 1982), indicated that privicy legislation was to be enacted in 1983.

NCC is now undertaking with French and German counterparts, Agence de l'Informatique (ADI) and GMD, a Data Security and Confidentiality study for the EEC, following earlier studies, which will examine and support the study of:

— the need for harmonisation of legislation, recommendations and standards on privacy;

— the improved control of computer data security including its technical feasibility and financial implications;

— an improved insight into the impact of privacy and security measures;

taking into account recent developments in the area of telematics and
their environment. The study will investigate the following items:

— new information and communication technologies and data protection;

— data protection and data security technology;

— data protection implications of personal profiles and automated
decision-making;

— the impact of international data protection regulations on special
information-intensive sectors of industry;

— system design and data protection;

— freedom of information and data protection;

— databases, distributed systems and data protection.

A security measure which can be used for several purposes in computer
systems is data encryption, and this could be provided as an option in
office systems for organisations to use as appropriate (see also Bibliography, item 6.8). However the user/office system interface must be user-
friendly with the number of passwords and encryption keys which the
user must enter kept to a minimum, otherwise the user will become
confused about when to use each. A BSI Technical Committee (OIS/21)
commenced work in 1980 and is responsible for UK participation in the
work of the International Organisation for Standardisation (ISO) working group ISO/TC 97/WG 1 and for British standards for data encryption.
The current work of OIS/21 is concerned with:

— specifications for data encryption algorithms;

— methods of using encryption in data processing protocols;

— guidelines for the use of encryption including key management
and the impact of equipment design.

FILE SPACE ALLOCATION

On-line file storage costs have fallen and may be expected to continue to
do so, which means that it becomes easier for users to justify more on-line

file storage space than hitherto. Nevertheless office systems will continue, for some time, to offer end users only quite a limited volume of on-line storage space. The restriction is not only an economic one. It also concerns the limited capability of the text filing and retrieval routines offered with the systems. Many of these routines are efficient over only relatively low volumes of storage and beyond this limit can cause a degradation of system performance and unacceptably long response times.

When total storage is limited, its allocation to end users needs to be managed and some file space allocation policy needs to be adopted. Some approaches that can be taken are:

— allocate a fixed amount per end user and make that user responsible for the utilisation of that space;

— allocate a fixed amount per end user plus additional allocation for specific end-user needs;

— allocate public areas, for shared files and shared reference information, to identifiable groups of users; eg to departments;

— provide convenient-to-use procedures for archiving information from on-line storage to optical disk, microfilm, removable magnetic storage, etc.

When on-line file storage space is limited, end users need to be encouraged to be disciplined about what is to be kept on-line and what can be archived. For whereas Parkinson's Law states that work expands to fill the time available to do it in, it would seem reasonable to enunciate another law for the use of on-line file storage space: 'the amount of information stored on-line will expand to fill the space available'.

At Tulsa, Oklahoma the Amoco Production Company Research Centre introduced word processing in 1972 using an IBM magnetic tape and card system and audio dictation in a word processing centre (WPC) set up with a supervisor, 11 word processing operatives and an administrative clerk. In 1975 the WPC supervisor felt that the WPC was not really 'cutting the mustard' and suggested to the Manager of Computing Research that he found some way of using the Research Centre's IBM mainframe computer. During the period from 1975 to 1977 IBM 3270 type terminals were installed in the WPC, using the IBM Script text processing language, and then software was developed to allow IBM System 6 ink jet printers to be linked into the IBM 370 mainframe

168 PLANNING OFFICE AUTOMATION

computer system.

Late in 1977 the Manager of Computing Research, Mr James C Steward, started experimenting with software for an electronic office system. This software had been written for use with the IBM VM/CMS (virtual machine/conversational monitor system). By December 1980, when one of the authors (JATP) and a colleague Paul Wilson visited Tulsa for talks with Mr Steward, 575 terminals on the site were connected up to the mainframe by coaxial cables. About 325 professional workers, 200 technicians, supervisors and some others of the 700 employees at the site had terminals – a few had two. (NB About 500 of these terminals had been installed to give users access to the data processing services on the mainframe, particularly for scientific and technical work. The others were added to provide the critical mass of users which is necessary for electronic office benefits to be achieved and for the problem of dual systems to be avoided.)

Since the critical mass of users has been achieved, a rule has been introduced that a person shall not send a paper document to someone else when it is possible to use electronic means. Electronic filing is well established as a way of life at this site. In the Computing Research Department, two administrative secretaries support 61 managers and professionals and, freed of practically all typing (which goes to the WPC), they spend much of their time entering documents into the electronic filing system. Electronic filing has been so successful that no filing cabinets have had to be purchased for the 61 managers and professionals during the three-year-period, 1978 to 1980, following the introduction of the electronic office system. A centralised paper document filing system is held in the office of the two administrative secretaries for incoming letters, magazine clippings, etc (NB OCR and optical disk techniques for filing paper documents electronically are not being used at this time). The administrative secretaries create an entry in the electronic filing system for each paper document so that managers, professionals and technicians (ie MPT personnel) can search for themselves from their terminals when seeking a paper document stored in the centralised filing system or an electronic document.

Of course there are many documents stored electronically. In particular there are seven large manuals in the Large On-line Document System. For example, the Computers and Standards manual used to be updated six times a year and distributed to 530 people. This activity used one man year of effort per year (ie 1700 man hours a year) and it was not difficult to cost justify this application. The Electronic Office System manual describing how users may use the electronic office system is itself 100 A4 pages long, so over 50,000 A4 sheets were used to reprint it, not to mention paper used to notify users of updates.

Documents are stored on IBM 3350 disks (but IBM 3380 disks may be introduced in the future). During a visit to NCC in June 1981, Mr Steward reported that in nearly four years of operation, a total of 80,000 documents had been filed. These vary in size from less than one page up to 200 pages. Although all these documents could be held on one IBM 3350 disk, this would make response times slow, so 25 disks are used to speed up access and retrieval times. Once a document is filed electronically it is never destroyed nor archived. A user can however erase his ability to retrieve any document which he is entitled to retrieve if he chooses to do so.

This housekeeping activity brings a user two benefits. It reduces search times and it eliminates the retrieval of documents which are no longer of interest or which are out of date. This practice of course also speeds up response times for other users. Although magnetic tape archiving facilities exist, no documents have ever been archived. If this were done, a record of the existence of archived documents would still be available; the details of where the document was archived could be retrieved and then the archived document could be recovered. It is estimated that it was costing about $1 to store a one-page document in on-line file storage for three years. In a typical week of operation about 10,000 retrievals are performed (about 20 per person per week), compared with about 2000 accesses to the electronic telephone directory (about four per person per week).

INDEXES

Readers will be aware of the importance of good indexing systems for paper-based filing systems and for records in computer-based systems. They will have observed indexing systems in public and corporate libraries, and may have experience of data dictionary systems which hold information about the data that an organisation uses and processes. In the electronic office, electronic indexes will be used for paper-based filing systems and for electronic filing systems. Electronic indexing systems must be designed to be easy and convenient to use and help users to select and retrieve the documents and information which they need: otherwise users will become disillusioned, will revert to paper filing and indexing, and will miss out on the benefits of electronic filing and indexing.

Indexing is an area where an electronic information management system should be designed to suit the user's conceptual model of information, so that needs can be expressed in understandable terms and so that irrelevant information is not demanded.

NCC's Office and Communications Systems Division had not encountered difficulties or problems during the first six months usage of its local network electronic filing facilities, although this may have been due in part to the fact that its user community of 12 users is relatively small and there were not very many electronic files or documents.

A description follows of the indexing system used by one of the authors. (NB It should be pointed out firstly that the terminology used in this description differs from that used in the system documentation provided by the supplier organisation Zynar, and secondly that the authors do not wish readers to infer that they are recommending this indexing method – more research into and experience of the usage of alternative methods of indexing is called for.)

A single line description of each file is held in a file index file and a single line description of each filed electronic document is held in a document index file. This is illustrated in Figure 6.2. At the top is a description of each of the six electronic files which are named '/main/users/oxjatp/1' through to '/main/users/oxjatp/6/zynar'. This file index file is followed by a document index file for each of the six electronic files. Information retrieval and document updating in this electronic filing system is supported by software whose facilities include the ability to locate any specified word or string of characters, or any preset marker, within a specified electronic document – including the index. To date this system has been robust enough to handle user filing, but will probably need to be, and will be, refined in the next year as the number of filed documents grows, and as the amount of shared access filing grows. The use of keywords in the index is a possibility which will be considered.

The other author carried out research at Loughborough University (1977-1981) for his doctorate. This work was concerned with characterising the information which people store in their own memories when doing typical filing tasks, so as to make recommendations for designing

File index text   on /MAIN/USERS/OXJATP/1   Page 1   Tue 27 Apr
9:08

ELECTRONIC FILE INDEX
File   Description

/main/users/oxjatp/1   current and personal administration
/main/users/oxjatp/2   new project and miscellaneous
/main/users/oxjatp/3/oanews   filed messages (OA and admin) and documents
/main/users/oxjatp/4/ims   IMS project and book
/main/users/oxjatp/5/blend   electronic journal project
/main/users/oxjatp/6/zynar   network administration messages

ELECTRONIC DOCUMENT INDEXES
INDEX: file = /main/users/oxjatp/1

Document   Description

TICKLER   List of things to do
STARTCMD   System
PROFILE   System
SNAP   Format for snapshot report for Irene

JATPFILE   JATP's filing system index
LISA   Letter to Lisa re conference; 13 Oct 81
SUBMISSION   News about OX 82/85 AERB submission for funding
network   Note to JMC about network

BENEFITS   45705   How to access PROJPROP:BENEFITS
NEWS   45705   News item for NCC Interface; 5 Oct 81
BEN-NOTES   45705   Notes about how to do project; 15 Oct 81
BENREPORT   45705   Progress report; Jan 82 (see /m/u/oxpaw/benefits)
BENBOOK

TRAIN81
TRAIN

LEAVE   Leave taken 1982/83
TELEPHONE   Telephone and telex numbers and addresses
DIARY   diary of events 1982/83
PATHS   pathnames and filenames

FILES   snapshots of unused file space and files in use
CONNOR
TV
TV1

THANKS   letter to IMS book draft readers
PAUL
QWE
CONDON

INDEX2:   file = /main/users/oxjatp/2

NEC   NEC's Integrated Electronic PBX
JAPAN   John Youmans
BENMESS   comments on BENEFITS book draft
NEWPROJ 82   project description – inoexins of paper

Figure 6.2   Electronic Filing   – Indexing (See over)

File index text   on /MAIN/USERS/OXJATP/1   Page 2   Tue 27 Apr
9:08

IMSMESS   IMS messages 22 Jan 82 - 7 Apr 82

INDEX3:   file = /main/users/oxjatp/3/oanews

DANEWS   miscellaneous messages
DANEWS 1   miscellaneous messages
ADMIN   administrative messages

DIRECTOR   meeting with Director 2 March 1982
IRENE   documents held by Irene
PAUL   documents filed by PA Wilson

INDEX4:   file = /main/users/oxjatp/4/ims

IMSCONT   contents of book
IMS   messages
IMS2   messages
IANIMS   types of ims
IMSAIMS   aim of book

IMP   processes of OA
IMSPVSC   pros and cons
VIEWDATA   viewdata systems
DBIS&R   storage/retrieval implications
RELTEXT   relevant text

IMSSI   strategic issues
IMSDC   design considerations
QPR1   quarterly progress report, period 10 (5-1-82)
REPORT1   progress report OCT 81
QPR   progress report NOV 81

JE   essay on Japan
APPENDF   appendix F – useful address, IMS book
CHAP1.3   unused material, IMS book
LETTER   letter to IMS book reviewers

INDEX5:   file = /main/users/oxjatp/5/blend

PAPER1/81   paper 'The New Technology – A Professional's Reaction'
REPORT81   Electronic Journal project report for 1981
BLEND2   project news 22 DEC 1981

NEWS   project news 15 FEB 1982
NEWS1   Olivetti terminal

INDEX6:   file = /main/users/oxjatp/6/zynar

XYNAR1	network messages	23 Sep	81 – 16	Nov 81
ZYNAR2	" "	16 Dec	81 – 8	Jan 82
ZYNAR3	" "	22 Jan	82 – 8	Mar 82
ZYNAR4	" "	1 Mar	82 – 19	Apr 82
MAIL	misc. messages	18 Jan	82 – 16	Feb 82

Figure 6.2   Electronic Filing – Indexing (continued)

computer-based office systems.

He found that when using a conventional pigeon-hole system for filing, people developed a strong mental picture of the pigeon-holes, even when they were randomly arranged (see Figure 6.3A) which enabled them to find specific locations accurately and easily. (Each pigeon-hole represented a specific category of information and was labelled accordingly.) Alternatively, when they used random lists of the same category labels (see Figure 6.3B) as in a computer system their mental picture of the lists was weak. Their accuracy in locating the labels was poor compared with finding the pigeon-holes.

A person's inherent awareness of position works well in a normal three-dimensional environment, such as the office. However, this positional awareness is not so successful when one is confronted with a two-dimensional medium such as a VDU screen or computer printout.

The explanation is that there are many and varied cues (eg colour, shape, depth, size, relative positions) from which a person can build up a mental picture of the environment. However, when information is presented as a list on a flat surface (such as a VDU screen or printout), many of these cues are either not present or are less dominant, especially those associated with spatial position.

In the experiments, in order to compensate for this it was necessary to alter the characteristics of the random lists and to provide more cues. Further experiments showed that simply grouping descriptors (see Figure 6.3C) was not enough. They had to be grouped according to some meaningful relationships bringing together every one in a common class (see Figure 6.3D).

It seems therefore that in order to locate a descriptor in a list, where strong spatial cues for a vivid mental picture are absent, an individual's mental processes can develop an approach based on category relationships. For example, the subject might remember that the grouping at the top of an index list consists of the names of files containing details of commercial situations (see Figure 6.3D).

The implications are clear. Information should be displayed in lists with a clearly discernible structure so that we can form an appropriate mental model of displayed file names on which we can base our search.

It would seem that it would be worth while to take the trouble to design

A: Pigeon-hole array

Insurance	Stockbroking	Public transport	Journalism
Quality control	Banking	Engineering	Legal work
Environment	Local authority	Entertainment	Accountancy
Buying	Management services	Social work	Medical

B: Random List

Buying
Legal work
Entertainment
Accountancy
Medical
Social work
Local authority
Stockbroking
Quality control
Management services
Environment
Insurance
Public Transport
Engineering
Journalism
Banking
Civil Service
Industrial admin.
Advertising
Retailing
Hotel management
Catering

**C: Random list
spatially grouped**

Entertainment
Social work
Legal work
Insurance

Management services
Public transport
Journalism
Quality control

Engineering
Local authority
Buying
Stockbroking

Environment
Banking
Medical
Accountancy

Civil Service
Advertising
Retailing
Catering

**D: List with labels
grouped meaningfully**

Commerce
Accountancy
Banking
Insurance
Stockbroking

Industry
Buying
Engineering
Management services
Quality control

Public Services
Local authority
Medical
Public transport
Social work

Miscellaneous
Entertainment
Environment
Journalism
Legal work

Figure 6.3   Electronic Indexing   – User-Friendly Structure

and implement software into an office computer system which could
structure displayed information so that it can be easily understood and
enable users to find their required information easily.

WORKSTATIONS

(NB The reader is also referred to Section 4.2 of the EMS companion book; see Bibliography, item 1.3)

As expected, there have been significant improvements in recent years in the range of functions and ease-of-use of those items of electronic equipment which sit on an office worker's desk in front of his chair or on the horizontal flat surface of a piece of office furniture adjacent to his desk to which he turns by rotating the swivel chair. These machines used to be, and many in use still are, single-function equipments, eg:

— word processors;

— computer terminals;

— microcomputers;

— Prestel (or viewdata) terminals; etc.

But many are now multifunction machines, capable of performing several functions, such as:

— word processing;

— accessing a local site computer or, via a telephone line, a remote computer;

— personal computing;

— accessing Prestel and/or private viewdata systems;

— electronic mail;

— electronic filing;

— voice annotation of electronic documents;

— automatic conversion of electronic text to telex format;

— graphics generation; etc.

and therefore easier to justify because:

— an office worker can do a greater proportion of work at this equipment than was possible at any single-function machine;

— the total number of multifunction machines needed is less than the total number of single-function machines of various types, and therefore there are savings of office space and equipment cost.

Consequently, the tendency is to refer to these equipments, whether multi- or single-function, as workstations, because they are perceived as the electronic equipment which office workers use to do their work (and this is how they should be perceived;) rather than as function/application oriented machines. (See also Bibliography, items 6.9 and 6.10.)

Nevertheless, further improvements in functionality and ease of use must, and will, be made, accompanied by equipment pricing policies set by suppliers reflecting to a greater degree:

— prices that more user organisations can afford to pay;

— the increased likelihood of the user organisation justifying the expenditure;

— a reduced (perhaps two-year) pay-back period, (rather than a five- to seven-year payback period), so that users will not be afraid that they will be trapped with equipment made obsolete by new technological developments;

and to a lesser degree:

— the supplier's research and development costs;

— the supplier's uncertainty that he will be able to sell as many machines as he would like, because the market place is saturated with too many suppliers competing against each other – which is still true.

At this stage of the development of multifunction workstations, the following fuctions are of interest from the information management point of view:

— voice facilities (see also Bibliography, item 6.11);

— split screen operation;

— personal annotation;

— computer database/viewdata format.

There are the following types of voice facility which in theory could be offered in a workstation:

— recognition (user-dependent and/or user-independent) of a limited vocabulary of voice commands as an alternative to entering commands through the keyboard, because keying takes up slightly more time and requires one or both hands which might be needed for holding a telephone handset, writing or holding a book open at a certain page;

— voice annotation of electronic documents (the spoken words are stored and played back when required, there is no voice recognition and the speaker can talk naturally);

— natural language voice input (user-dependent and/or user-independent) of text as an alternative to keying by managers and professionals who generate text but are not proficient at touch typing (ie the majority of managers and professionals);

— voice output.

NB User-dependent voice recognition requires that the workstation has been programmed to know the voices of certain users who have registered with it. This is not the case with user-independent voice recognition which may operate with a smaller vocabulary.

Voice commands can be provided now and could be used (as an option) to move the cursor, to perform text and file editing functions, and to carry out other workstation housekeeping functions. However a user-friendly non-voice alternative for several of these functions is to select an option from a numbered menu list. Another alternative is to use a single or two-character abbreviation; managers, in particular, may find difficulty in finding the time to learn and in remembering these abbreviations – although this same problem arises if voice commands have to be learned and remembered because it may be a long time before a standard voice command language is developed and adopted.

One of the authors has seen voice command features successfully used in a demonstration (of a system for training airline pilots at Boeing Computer Services, Seattle, Washington) and has heard of their use for quality control and information management relating to assembly operations and of their possible use by USA air traffic controllers. He has not heard of their use in an office environment yet, though it probably exists in some USA companies. The quality control and assembly applications are of interest and relevance to OA because they indicate how voice commands could easily be used with benefit in the office. In another USA aircraft manufacturing company, 30% of a quality controller's time was taken up by writing data manually onto five different forms when a test failed. When the voice system was installed, it became possible to collect data for all tests undertaken. In yet another USA aircraft manufacturing company, the parts in a board assembly operation were controlled by the assemblers entering information on forms which travelled with the boards. The computer eventually got hold of the information but often not until three months later. When this system was replaced by a voice input system using 17 voice entry stations and costing $600,000, the assemblers were free to use both hands for assembling uninterrupted by periods of writing information by hand on to forms. In the first year of the voice system, savings were estimated at $470,000 and there was also the unquantified benefit of having information available earlier for better planning.

Voice annotation is now available in, for example, the Office Technology Limited's (OTL) Information Management Processor (I.M.P.) Principal Workstation and is likely to be provided by many more suppliers as an easy-to-learn and use option for electronic document annotation. Natural language voice input is nearer than many people realise and for this we must congratulate the Japanese. At the Data Show 81 exhibition in Tokyo in October 1981 the authors saw a word processor being controlled by voice commands and predict major developments in this field in Japan before the end of 1984. Indeed the research and development of the fifth generation computer systems aims to develop a phonetic typewriter which can:

— handle 10,000 words with simultaneous meaning analysis;

— perform automatic error correction during speech recognition;

— generate comprehensible sentences;

and a speech-responding system which can:

— handle 10,000 words;

— comprehend the meaning of questions to be answered;

— carry on natural conversation.

It is interesting to note that in November 1981 Logica announced a product, Logos automatic speech system, developed in conjunction with the government's Joint Speech Research Unit, which performs continuous voice recognition from a vocabulary of 2000 words. Voice output, of course, is not a problem and many voice output systems are in use for various purposes. However office workers may not require a facility for the output of computer-generated responses (we are not referring to the delivery of spoken messages from humans which have been stored and forwarded), when these can be visually displayed on a screen. (NB Some office workers cannot concentrate on creative thinking if they are within earshot of colleagues who are talking to visitors, or talking on the telephone, and OA planners must heed this point prior to the appearance of electronic booths which will avoid this problem.)

An important workstation design feature is split screen operation. This is desirable as users begin to migrate from paper-based methods of working to mixed electronic/paper methods and will become essential as more and more information migrates to electronic form. This is because as a user is, say, creating text for a report at his workstation he will SIMULTANEOUSLY want to display this text and other text which contains information which he wishes to use in his draft and which he has retrieved for temporary display, such as electronic messages, electronically-filed minutes, and electronically-filed notes of meetings, telephone conversations and articles. Without split-screen operation, a user's creative thinking will be disturbed and the quality of his work impaired if he has to alternate between different displays on the screen, and he may revert to taking hard copies. Most people say that it is unnatural not to work with documents spread out on one's desk (and sometimes on the floor too) – and this is certainly how the authors work at the present time!

Users should demand, and suppliers should provide, split-screen operation: it is a key design issue in bringing the full benefits of OA. Indeed, the multifunction workstation of the future must provide an easy-to-operate facility for the screen to be partitioned in different ways into two or more portions of different shapes, with the corresponding displayed information temporarily enlarged or reduced in size. It should be possible also to temporarily remove displayed information from the screen and recall it by pressing a single key – not just contiguous passages of text from the same document, but to alternate between passages from different documents.

The personal annotation facility for voice has been mentioned above, but there is also clearly a need for a workstation to allow a user to annotate an electronic document, as one does a paper document, by writing notes in the margin. There should be an option for annotating the user's personal copy only, as well as an option for annotating the public copy of the document. (In a few years' time, a user will not only be able to add marginal notes but also to mark up the electronic document itself with some words crossed out, with some words underlined or circled, or with arrows transferring text to a new position. The workstation (or the computer to which it is attached) will be able to infer the wishes of the user and to present him with amended text just as if a typist had amended the document through her keyboard.) One other useful annotation facility is highlighting.

Personal annotation can be entered through the keyboard but many users who will need this facility will wish to have the option to use:

— voice commands;

— light pen;

— touching the screen;

— writing tablet.

Users will need to access information held in viewdata format and in computer databases (using a retrieval command language). There are developments in hand here too to:

— use gateways (ie software) to allow Prestel and other viewdata systems to route enquiries to databases on other computers;

— allow one enquiry to initiate a search of several databases (Euronet-DIANE);

— allow information held in databases to be reformatted in viewdata format (eg Langton Information Systems Preview software, Debenham's Viewbase and (see below) the CEC study for Euronet-DIANE);

— allow workstations to access both computer databases and view-databases.

At present, users of Prestel and other viewdata information services cannot access Euronet-DIANE hosts and databases because neither the Euronet network nor the host computers can accept the characters generated on a viewdata terminal (ie a normal TV set with an adaptor). A study by Télésystèmes showed that interworking would be desirable and technically possible. It would probably not be practical to transfer the databases to viewdata computers because the tree-structure search is not fast enough for huge files of hundreds of thousands of records, and the viewdata terminal screen limitation of 30 to 40 characters per display row, compared with 80 characters or more on teletype-compatible terminals and intelligent terminals, imposes severe limits on the quantity of information and its layout, particularly tabular information.

The CEC has set up a study to deal with this problem by looking at the transmission of data between a Euronet-DIANE host computer and a viewdata terminal, viz:

— the creation of data by the host in a form suitable for presentation on a viewdata terminal;

— the conversion of data into viewdata terminal message formats;

— the design of a suitable set of parameters, or network conventions, which can be added to present Euronet switching equipment.

For many users an attraction of viewdata is its ease of use for managers and non-computer-oriented personnel who would prefer not to have to learn and to remember one, or several, command languages to use an information retrieval system to search for and retrieve information from a database. Another is the low cost of the adapted TV set which serves as the user's viewdata system terminal. (Viewdata terminals are basically adapted TV sets which can display characters of variable dimensions and colours, and which have extended facilities for graphics. A teletype-compatible VDU will not have these facilities, although more expensive intelligent terminals and microcomputer workstations may have.) Many large computer databases cannot be stored in viewdata format because it is not practical to use a viewdata type of tree-structured search. Therefore a viewdata terminal on its own can only be useful up to a point for an office worker and he would need another workstation for all his other needs – other than retrieving information from viewdata systems. But the cost of two machines per office worker is difficult to justify, both because of the actual costs involved and because at any moment in time at least one of the two machines would probably not be in use. Hence the impetus for multifunction workstations (which include viewdata capability, because of the importance of this type of information retrieval system), because:

— one workstation takes up less desk space than two (and some office workers grumble about the size and weight of a single workstation, which preferably ought not to be very much bigger and heavier than an Apple II microcomputer);

— one workstation would be less expensive than two, less sophisticated, workstations;

— one workstation should have a higher utilisation than the average utilisation of two, less sophisticated (ie having less functions), workstations and therefore the investment in it should be easier to justify.

An example of a currently-available workstation which has this capability is the Teleputer (formerly the System Alpha) of Rediffusion Computers Limited. It can be used as:

— a computer terminal;

— a word processor;

— a computer-assisted learning system;

— a mail-order catalogue;

— a remote-batch terminal;

— a local microcomputer (it has 64K byte memory and twin floppy disk storage);

— a viewdata/videotex terminal;

— a colour graphics computer;

— a colour television set.

An interesting development is the office viewdata telephone; this is a combined telephone and viewdata terminal; (it can also be used at home). In 1980 Plessey announced the Plessey Vutel which has $5\frac{1}{2}$-inch white characters on a black background display of 24 lines by 40 characters. Its dimensions are 30 cm (11.8 in) wide, 31 cm (12.2 in) deep, and 16 cm (6.3 in) high, weighing 5 kg (11 lbs). It has been designed so that subsequently further facilities can be added such as:

— printer and cassette interfaces;

— abbreviated dialling;

— alphanumeric keyboard and note-pad (it has at present a numeric keypad and function keys);

— call cost and metering;

— alarm, time and number displays;

— call timer.

Vutel was shown at the Viewdata 81 exhibition in October 1981, which also featured similar devices from GEC, Philips, and Intelmatique, the French information technology products supplier.

STANDARDS

Many user organisations have expressed serious concern about the lack of standards in several areas which affect OA, often mentioning it as a major consideration affecting their progression towards the integrated electronic office. The reason for this concern is that a proliferation of non-standard hardware, software, communications protocols, local area networks, user/system interfaces, etc, makes it impossible, difficult or costly to integrate different components and systems of the electronic office. It therefore complicates strategic planning, makes justification more difficult and increases the amount of learning for users. Although most organisations say that standards activity should be intensified and speeded up, many are not willing to support the work of standards-making organisations because they cannot justify the cost of the deployment of their manpower resources in this way – although the benefit to them as users of the availability of agreed standards may be many times greater than this cost.

Ever since its birth in 1966, NCC has tried to raise the level of awareness of the benefits to users of the development of standards and has supported the work of BSI and other organisations. Much of NCC's thrust in standards work in the 1970s came from former colleague Ray O'Connor who led the team which produced the 1977 *Report on Standards in Computing* and who received the 1977 Fred Butcher Memorial Award from the British Standards Society. NCC's Standardisation Office has expanded its work programme recently and provides a free information service on the content of computing standards of all types; it also holds reference copies. Some important developments are taking place at present in several standards areas relevant to OA. Any detailed information given here could very quickly become out-of-date and readers are advised to make contact with NCC's Standardisation Office when they require current information. This Office has published more than 20 reports in its 'Guides to Computing Standards' series, in particular (see Bibliography, item 6.12):

— *The Making of Standards* (a useful overview of the standards-making process which also explains the roles of the many different organisations active in the standards field);

— *Automation in Bibliography* (this report refers to nine BSI and six ISO standards; it was prepared by Mr Alan Hopkinson who has participated in a number of working groups of ISO technical committee TC 46 Documentation);

— *Keyboard Layouts* (this report refers to five BSI standards, including one draft standard, and to five ISO standards; it was prepared by Mr Hugh McGregor Ross who was a member of BSI technical committee DPE/7 Keyboard Layouts and for seven years Chairman of DPS/-, BSI's Industry Standards Committee, responsible for all British standardisation work for computers and data processing and for UK contributions to ISO work; NB DPS (Data Processing Systems) committees were renamed OIS (Office and Information Systems) committees by BSI in 1980);

— *Microfilm and Microfiche* (this report refers to seven BSI standards, and one draft standard, and to three ISO standards; it was prepared by Kathleen Oldham who has served on BSI technical committee OMS/12 Banking Procedures for several years).

Copies of the standards referred to in these reports may be obtained from BSI's sales organisation, (see Useful Addresses, item 6.1).

Elsewhere in this book, mention has been made of other standards work which is being undertaken or is desirable. Areas of current relevance to OA include:

— open systems interconnection (see Bibliography, items 6.13 and 6.14);

— local area networks (see Bibliography, items 6.15, 6.16 and 6.17);

— keyboards (see Bibliography, item 6.12);

— information retrieval command languages;

— viewdata (see Bibliography, item 6.18).

LOCATION OF INFORMATION

Information stored in viewdata systems tends to be short life information which the information provider deletes or updates regularly, some of it daily. We have evidence of this from NTT in Japan who report that (at October 1981) Captain held 140,000 frames of information, although 440,000 had been created since Captain began operation; so about two-thirds of the frames have been deleted or updated. Information stored on databases, particularly on-line bibliographic databases, tends to be of long life (and therefore suitable for storage on optical disks). New information is added to existing files; existing information is not deleted. 1982 trade figures do not replace 1981 trade figures; statistics for successive years are retained so that trends can be identified and reasons for these trends investigated. For such massive files, the viewdata type of tree-structured search is inappropriate and direct keyword access or a CAFS-type search is necessary.

7 The Future

NATIONAL STRATEGIC PLANNING

This book and the complementary book for EMS (see Bibliography, item 1.3) have addressed the subject of OA strategic planning at a corporate level. But should a country's government have a policy and a strategic plan for information technology? This subject, interesting and important in its own right, is also of relevance to corporate OA strategic planning if there is some truth in the view put to us by several people that it would raise awareness, help UK suppliers meet the threat from abroad, help identify markets, co-ordinate investment policies, and make better use of resources.

The Japanese JIPDEC FGCS project came under international scrutiny in October 1981 and the UK government's Department of Industry and the EEC are known to be considering how to respond to this initiative and whether to offer the co-operation sought by the Japanese. However FGCS is looking forward to 1990 and beyond; what about the 1980s?

One of the authors of this book addressed an audience at the Sheffield City Polytechnic in October 1978 on the subject of new technology; the title of that talk was 'Some thoughts on the effects of the technological developments upon people in the computing industry and society in general'. One prediction at that talk was that viewdata would become a most important piece of information management technology during the early 1980s. Another prediction concerned the role of the government. It was forecast that it would not be at the next general election in the UK (which occurred in May 1979), nor at the following one (which must occur no later than May 1984), but at the one following that when the electorate will demand to know from the political parties what their policies are towards new technology and the consequential employment, redeployment and retraining, and unemployment issues and will treat these policies as a major election issue. It is vital, therefore, that the 'man in the street', unions, employers, the retired, the unemployed and others should be aware of the types of impact that new technology will have upon work and leisure, and be interested in and competent to discuss the merits of alternative national strategies.

The relevance of unemployment, and the related unused human resources that this represents, to office automation is that:

— it highlights the need for investment in new technology to remain competitive, and to create jobs and the wealth to support public sector services;

— it highlights the problems associated with the introduction of new technology, problems which are probably greater in the UK than they need have been because of a lack of awareness and a reluctance to change which have caused many UK companies to become relatively uncompetitive vis-a-vis foreign rivals or to go out of business.

The lack of awareness in the UK of the opportunities offered by new technology and of the importance of seizing those opportunities contrasts sharply with the positive attitudes towards new technology in general and office automation in particular found by the authors in Japan in October 1981. The Japanese perceive new technology as their friend – as something which creates jobs and enables them to produce high-quality manufactured goods which are in demand throughout the world and pay for the essential imports of oil and food. Japanese industrial relations also contrast sharply with those found in the UK. A Japanese company's management and its employees often have a relationship based on trust, full consultation, a lifelong commitment to look after each other, etc. New technology changes jobs. In Japan, workers are redeployed and retrained; in the UK companies and unions enter into new technology agreements with no compulsory redundancy clauses but a net reduction in jobs, apparently complacent to maintain present production levels more cost-effectively.

Many people in the UK have never heard of office automation; many of those who have perceive of it as word processors which increase the productivity of typists, quite unaware of the opportunities to use new technology to help managers, professionals, clerks and secretaries too. But it is not just individuals, but also companies at whom criticism has been levelled. The Minister for Information Technology, Mr Kenneth Baker, is reported (see Bibliography, item 7.1) to have said in the House of Commons in December 1981 'It is depressing that, despite all the effects of this and the previous Government, 50% of UK companies still do not use microtechnology . . . Many industries, whether manufacturing furniture, biscuit tins, carpets or clothing, must use the new technologies or they will not be in business in the next five or ten years'.

Rising unemployment, Japanese imports, IT82 . . . pressure is building up for politicians, managers, unions, employees, shareholders, academics, local government, etc, to co-operate in the development and execution of a national strategy to identify, and make and use products and systems based on new technology . . . but first they must perceive that there is a problem. Government IT schemes announced or operational at the end of 1981 included:

— IT82;

— micros in schools, (a £4 million scheme to ensure that all secondary schools have a microcomputer – a Research Machines RML380Z or an Acorn 'BBC' microcomputer – by the end of 1982 by giving local authorities 50% grant aid);

— Microelectronics in Education Programme (MEP);

— Information Technology Centres (Itecs);

— eight pilot electronic office schemes for public sector users;

— microprocessor applications project (MAP);

— microelectronic industry support programme (MISP);

— support for fibre optics, opto-electronics and industry robotics;

— £77M support for the L-Sat communications satellite project.

Despite all this support and activity, there has been criticism that the government should have had a national strategic plan for IT and taken the initiative instead of, apparently, just making tactical *ad hoc* responses, and that IT82 was 'more a shield for inaction than a catalyst for development' (see Bibliography, items 7.2 and 7.3).

Three bodies, the EEC, NEDO and the National Electronics Council, should be mentioned. JEPE-IT (Joint European Planning Exercise in Information Technologies) is an exercise supported by the Commission of the European Communities and led by Viscount Etienne Davignon, Vice-President of the Commission and Commissioner with responsibilities for industry and research. It will lay the basis for a Community-wide programme of work which will form the response to the Japanese FGCS initiative (and could embrace co-operation and collaboration with the Japanese). A National Economic Development Office (NEDO) working party report from its Electronics Economic Development Committee (see Bibliography, items 7.4 and 7.5) claimed that the UK has a very modest programme of government support for the electronic components industry and called for the development of an overall strategy to match the long-term industrial planning and preproduction investment of the Japanese. This report (see Bibliography, item 7.6) was published in April 1982 by NEDO and is seen by many people who have read it as a major milestone in strategic planning for information technology.

A National Electronics Council (NEC) report (see Bibliography, item 7.7) was produced in 1981 by a NEC working party 'On Adapting to the Information Society', under the chairmanship of Professor J D Rhodes of the University of Leeds. Its terms of reference were: 'To draw the attention of the appropriate sections of Government, Public and Private Industry, Trade Unions and Educational Authorities to the importance and social impact of electronics and software engineering, as applied to information and control technology, and to the priority these should enjoy; and to make recommendations by early 1981 on the actions that might be taken to enable the United Kingdom to benefit from the new technology'. The NEC report noted that 'France and Japan have plans for adapting their internal systems to take advantage of the industrial opportunities now being opened by the use of high technology, and that 'the UK has resources in technical ability and finance to tackle successfully, if properly organised, what is probably the greatest single industrial opportunity of this century', and called for the UK to introduce a national plan 'to bring about a change in the attitude to the creation of wealth, to make education more effective, and to provide incentives for innovation and development'.

TECHNOLOGICAL DEVELOPMENTS AND CONSEQUENCES

This book has discussed the strategic issues and design considerations which an OA strategy for a user organisation should address with respect to the nine types of IMS listed in Appendix C. It is based upon products and systems (many of them imported) available in the UK now, or likely to become available in the next year or two, and upon current office practices.

Technological developments will occur at a fast rate during the next decade and will increase the functionality, user-friendliness and cost-effectiveness of multifunction workstations. These developments will be in hardware (storage capacity, processing power, storage access mechanisms), chips, software, telecommunications and value-added services.

Optical disks, optical-fibre transmission, OCR, the BT System X programme and digital network programme, communications satellites, voice recognition, VLSI chips and ULSI chips (ultra large scale integration circuits with between 10 million and 100 million gates per chip) and other developments will transform the products and systems available for the electronic office, affecting dramatically current office practices.

Developments in chip technology will be particularly important, for chips are key elements which will improve the performance and functionality of workstations in the electronic office, and of the computers to which the workstations are connected through local area networks. 16K bit RAM memory chips are commonplace to-day, while 64K bit RAM memory chips are becoming widely used in products such as the Fujitsu M380 computer marketed by ICL. Indeed a very competitive battle has been joined by several companies in Japan and in the USA and it is reported that Japanese companies have captured about 70% of the 64K RAM market (ie chips which store 64,000 bits).

At the International Solid State Circuits Conference (ISSCC) in San Francisco in February 1982 (see Bibliography, item 7.8) the latest developments in 256K memory chips using CMOS and NMOS technology were announced. High access speeds are achieved by reducing the distance between circuits from three or four microns to about one micron; some laboratories are achieving sub-micron circuitry. One of the first developments of 256K chips was a joint venture by the two Japanese companies NEC (Nippon Electric Company) and Toshiba Corporation who produced samples in September 1981 – an output from the successful Japanese national VLSI project. An announcement was made at the ISSCC by Hewlett-Packard that they have produced for internal use a six chip 32-bit minicomputer. This is an important step in the direction of providing the power of a mainframe computer within an office desk top workstation. The machine, the 'six chip set', has six devices: a CPU, a memory controller, a 128K RAM memory unit based on a VLSI chip containing 660,000 semiconductor devices, a ROM unit, an input/output processor and a clock generator. Early in 1982, Toshiba announced plans to develop samples of a one megabit RAM chip in 1983 with full-scale production during 1984/85.

Paper flows will migrate to electronic messaging, paper files will migrate to electronic filing, keyboarding will migrate to voice input and OCR. New forms of communication will become possible – for example, teleconferencing with voice, text and image, both in simultaneous mode (ie people at different sites conferring with each other as though they were all present in the same room) and in non-simultaneous mode.

In this latter mode anyone who is a participant in such a teleconference will be able at any time to bring to a workstation any of the filed voice, text and image contributions and then enter a contribution into the filing system. For example, the user might be a manager or professional or knowledge worker in an office in Manchester who listens to a conversation between two colleagues or business associates which took place a few hours earlier in a Tokyo office. Not only does he listen to the recorded, filed and retrieved conversation, but it is also possible to see the participants and diagrams which they have drawn or annotated. In both modes of teleconferencing, participants will be able to retrieve quickly and conveniently any form of information (voice, text, data, graphics or image) stored in any public database anywhere in the world.

The electronic office has been described as a paperless office: paper pollution will first be checked and then brought under control. Paper-based attitudes to office work are deeply entrenched in most senior managers and many other employees, but these attitudes will change as people see the benefits of office automation. Legislation will be needed to give electronic documents the legal status enjoyed at present only by paper documents. International co-operation will ensure that international trade can take full advantage of office systems technology.

Within 10 or 20 years, it will become a normal office practice for electronic documents to be printed only for transient use, eg for someone to work with while on a train or airplane journey; after a few hours, occasionally after a few days the need for the hard copy will no longer be present and it will be thrown away – or shredded, if confidential. The authors can see no situations in which such hard copy would find its way into paper-based filing systems – but although some leading-edge companies will operate like this within five years, in many more it will take at least a decade to happen.

It is frequently said that the office of the future will be a system rather than a place, that office workers will tend to do more work from home, assuming that they have electronic office facilities provided there. It will become increasingly attractive for office workers to be spared the cost and trouble of commuting to work every day and for organisations to redeploy that resource which is one of its most important after its employees, namely space. These two forces may generate a great growth industry in the 1980s and 1990s – electronic booths.

People will not in fact want to work at home, because it is the wrong environment but they will walk a few hundred yards and hire time at a booth. The hire charge will depend upon how many hours the person books the booth for, what services and functions the multifunction workstation in the selected booth supports and what use is made of these services. A person might spend three hours in the booth, spending half-an-hour dealing with electronic mail, half-an-hour interrogating public and corporate databases, an hour keying in the draft for a report and an hour preparing electronic 'visuals' for a lecture. After a two-hour lunch break, he might spend two more hours in the booth. Twice a week he might work like this, twice a week he might visit his office, and once a week he might travel to a meeting.

Many professional workers and managers spend about £3 a day on travelling from their home to their office and back again; some spend less, many spend more if they work in the metropolitan areas of Greater London or other large conurbations. Figure 7.1 illustrates what £3 currently buys in telephone time. In the future, the cost of travel may rise faster than the cost of using the telephone. Whether this occurs or not, the use of booths will probably grow because they will allow office workers to make better use of their time and to do much of their work more effectively.

Most office workers, because they will spend two days a week 'at the office' instead of five, will no longer have their own office with a desk, a telephone, a filing cabinet, a coat/hat stand, a bookcase and a piece of carpet. At the office, also, there will be many booths for personal work, and varying sizes of electronic offices for group work. Senior managers,

	Cheap rate		Standard rate		Peak rate	
	h	m	h	m	h	m
Local calls	8	00	2	00	1	30
Calls up to 35 miles	2	24		45		30
Calls over 35 miles		48		13		10

Key: h hours

   m minutes

   peak rate 0900 to 1300 hours (Monday to Friday)

   standard rate 0800 to 0900 hours, and 1300 to 1800 hours (Monday to Friday)

   cheap rate all other times

Figure 7.1   PSTN Telephone Time Bought for £3 (March 1982)

members of administrative support centres, members of the corporate
word processing centre, and other support staff (eg in the information
centre) will have their own rooms. Junior managers, professionals and
other knowledge workers will not have their own rooms. Before each visit
to the office, these people will have to make arrangements to book
booths, electronic offices, ASC services and other resources which they
need, but the actual making of these arrangements will be a quick,
convenient and trivial task – because of the electronic office facilities. The
resystematisation of office practices and procedures involved is considerable and will evolve gradually.

A senior manager in a leading Japanese company supplying OA products and systems explained the dilemma which suppliers may face: 'We
can identify the products and systems which users want, and we can
sooner or later develop the technology to a point where we can make
office machines which can do almost anything that users want them to do.
In the past, the pay-back period for a machine was reached long before
the machine was made obsolete by new technology. But technology is
changing so fast now. What marketing strategy should suppliers adopt if

in the future a machine becomes obsolete before its pay-back period is reached?' This dilemma faces users too as part of the OA strategic planning/investment decision process. In one UK company in 1982, the O and M (Organisation and Methods) Manager who had been given responsibility for OA strategic planning reported to us that the payback periods for word processors and microcomputers have been reduced to two years and one year respectively.

FIFTH-GENERATION COMPUTER SYSTEMS

The authors attended the international conference on Fifth-Generation Computer Systems (FGCS) in Tokyo during 19-22 October 1981. The conference, attended by 325 persons, was organised by JIPDEC (Japan Information Processing Development Centre) and supported by the Japanese Government's Ministry of International Trade and Industry (MITI). JIPDEC in Japan is perhaps the organisation whose role is closer to that of the NCC than is that of any other Japanese organisation. Like NCC, JIPDEC is a non-profit organisation and was established in 1967 with the support of government and industry to promote information processing industries in Japan and research and development of information processing technology.

Since 1979 a team of experts drawn from industry and universities, under the chairmanship of Professor Tohru Moto-oka of the University of Tokyo, has been carrying out studies on the establishment of objectives and research and development themes and plans concerning fifth-generation computer systems. This activity is an important JIPDEC project. The purpose of the 1981 FGCS conference was to present the team's work and, through invited papers and panel discussions, to bring together workers in this field from other countries to exchange views.

It is anticipated that fifth generation computer systems (see Figure 7.2) in the 1990s will be knowledge information processing systems (KIPS) and will be expected to play the following social roles:

— to increase productivity in low productivity areas, (eg offices);

— to meet international competition and contribute toward international co-operation;

— to assist in saving energy and resources (NB this is particularly important in Japan which spends massive sums of money on oil imports);

First-generation computers

— valve-driven machines (eg LEO 1)

Second-generation computers

— transistor-based machines (eg IBM 1401)

Third-generation computers

— integrated circuit machines (eg IBM S/360, ICL 1900)

— high-level programming languages (eg COBOL and FORTRAN)

— sophisticated operating systems (eg IBM OS, ICL GEORGE 3)

Fourth-generation computers

— VLSI technology-based machines (eg IBM 3081, Fujitsu M380)

— high-level programming languages (eg PASCAL, COBOL)

Fifth-generation computers

— new advanced technology

— new programming languages (eg PROLOG, LISP)

— new input methods (eg voice recognition, pattern recognition)

— artificial intelligence

— 1991 target for prototype machine

Figure 7.2   Progress Towards Fifth-Generation Computer Systems

— to cope with an aged society.

These are the issues which are expected to be dominant in Japanese society in the 1990s, but would seem to be very relevant to the UK too.

These KIPS systems will support machine translation of one natural language to another, medical diagnosis and economic analysis through human-oriented input/output capabilities such as voice, charts and drawings. These systems will become possible because of technological developments, which are certainly taking place in the very advanced research and development laboratories in Japanese companies, in such areas as:

— VLSI (very large scale integration);

— larger capacity memories;

— high speed elements;

— artificial intelligence;

— pattern recognition;

— the convergence of telecommunications and computing.

The FGCS project is a ten-year project, which is aiming to develop the basic technology by 1984 (the initial stage), complete the final research by 1988 (the intermediate stage) and develop a prototype fifth-generation computer system by 1991 (the final stage). The relevance of the Japanese FGCS project to office automation is that, amongst other objectives, it will seek to make Japan the world's leading supplier and user of electronic office systems.

It is outside the scope of this book to go into the mass of published details of the plans for fifth-generation computer systems and interested readers are referred to articles in Computing Europe and Computer Weekly or to JIPDEC for the proceedings of the FGCS conference (see Useful addresses, item 7.3) (see also Bibliography, items 7.9, 7.10, 7.11 and 7.12).

Some people – in the UK, Japan and elsewhere – have expressed scepticism about the possibility of developing all of the hardware and software components necessary for fifth-generation computer systems (knowledge information processing systems), about the practicability of integrating these into cost-effective systems, and about society's capacity to adapt to the consequential changes to long-established patterns of work and social behaviour – and one must respect these views. But such is the degree of commitment of the Japanese in a rapidly-changing environment that we should be wary of saying what is or is not possible or practical.

The JIPDEC FGCS project may or may not achieve all of its objectives within the proposed timescales and budgets, but is certain to generate outputs relevant to the long-range plans and strategies of UK suppliers and users of OA systems. In the USA, the USSR and Western

Europe, there is huge research and development expenditure on defence projects, leading to a large technology transfer spin-off into non-defence products, projects and applications. It may be significant that Japan's investment goes directly into non-defence research and development and that there is consequently a much faster transfer of technology into non-defence products, projects and applications.

A UK delegation led by Mr Reay Atkinson, at that time Head of the Department of Industry's Information Technology Division, attended the FGCS conference. Subsequently the UK Minister for Information Technology announced that the DoI, SERC, industry and academics would be meeting to draw up a work programme in the FGCS area. A first conference, called by DoI, was attended by 70 UK computing industry leaders in January 1982 to discuss the UK response (see Bibliography, items 7.13 to 7.16). In April 1982 it was announced (see Bibliography, item 7.17) that the UK government had set up a special study group to examine the scope for collaborative information technology research projects in such areas as:

— advanced software;

— man/machine interface;

— computer-aided design;

— interconnection of networks.

This body, the Alvey Committee, produced its report in the autumn of 1982.

Appendix A

Use of the Telecommunications Network*

INTRODUCTION

1 This guide is aimed principally at all individuals or organisations interested in making use of the British Telecommunications (BT) network to provide telecommunications value added network services (VANS) on a commercial basis, and explains the licensing procedure which was adopted by the Department of Industry on 1 April 1982.

2 It was announced last July that the Government's policy under the British Telecommunications Act 1981 would be to allow the private sector much greater freedom to use BT's inland network, thereby enabling the growing demand for more sophisticated telecommunications services to be satisfied more quickly than at present. It is hoped that this note will encourage private sector organisations to consider the possibilities for use of the UK's telecommunications network and to come forward with licence applications for new services.

ELIGIBILITY FOR LICENCES

3 It is already possible for some telecommunications services to be provided other than by BT without any licence if the running of such services has been exempted from BT's monopoly by the BT Act, eg services provided within a single legal entity.

4 From 1 April 1982, however, it will be possible for private organisations under licence to provide for any customer a wide range of

* Reprinted with permission of the Department of Industry.

services using BT's network, whether or not similar services are provided by BT or anyone else. Under this new policy all value added services as defined in paragraph 5 below, apart from international services, will be eligible for a licence, but those involving the straightforward resale of capacity on BT's network will not be eligible.

DEFINITION OF VALUE ADDED SERVICES

5   As far as the definition of value added services is concerned the intention is that any service which adds genuine value to, and contains substantial elements additional to the basic network, will be eligible. As a guide for applicants the following criteria will be used as part of the consideration of whether a proposed service should be licensed. A value added service is one which allows information to be interchanged directly between users of the service but not without first being:

   a. stored by the value added operator for the purpose of being subsequently retrieved or forwarded;
   or
   b. processed by the value added operator in such a way that when delivered the messages have been clearly altered as to format, protocol or content.

6   Since 'value added' services will continue to develop in line with the rapid advances in information technology and telecommunications systems, the above guidelines will be interpreted in a flexible way. The availability of general licences is being considered to cover particular types of service.

EXAMPLES OF ELIGIBLE VALUE ADDED SERVICES

7   The range of eligible services is already wide. There follows an illustrative list:

   Personal telephone answering services
   Personal message services
   Facsimile and other bureaux
   Viewdata
   Mailbox
   Store and forward telex services with additional facilities

Store and forward message switching with additional facilities
Protocol conversion between incompatible computers and terminals
Telesoftware storage and retrieval service
Automatic ticket reservation and issuing service.

HOW TO APPLY FOR A LICENCE

8   Applications for a licence should be made to Mr Ian Sibbick at the Department of Industry, Ashdown House, 123 Victoria Street, London SW1E 6RB. All applications should include general information about the proposed system, details of who will be running the system, the services which will be available, who will have access to the service and the type of equipment to be used. In particular, applications should explain clearly the storage and processing elements and their relative importance to the service as a whole.

ADVISORY PANEL

9   The Secretary of State has appointed an independent panel of three experts to advise him on general issues of licensing policy and in cases where applications do not exactly match the criteria. The panel consists of the following:

—   Professor Kenneth Cattermole (Chairman), Professor of Telecommunications at Essex University. He has been an adviser to the Department of Industry for three years.

—   Professor Brian Carsberg, Arthur Andersen Professor of Accounting at the London School of Economics.

—   Mr Stephen Finch, Chairman of the Telecommunications Managers Association, and Senior Regulatory Affairs Adviser at BP. Previously he was Group Communications Manager at BP for 12 years.

ATTACHMENTS

10   It is important to note that, under the British Telecommunications Act 1981, before any private apparatus is used in connection with BT maintained circuits or apparatus, it must be approved to ensure technical compatibility and safety. BT maintains lists of approved equipment which may be inspected at your local British Telecom

Area Office. Over the next three years, independent standards are being introduced as part of the Government's liberalisation programme; but where such standards have not been published and approved, the apparatus may be approved by BT. If the equipment has to be evaluated to ensure it meets the necessary requirements, BT will make a charge to cover the expense of the testing.

RADIO LINKS

11   Where the VANS involves an extension over a radio link, a separate licence for the use of the radio frequencies must be obtained from the Home Office.

ENQUIRIES

12   Any enquiries about this guide should be made to Ian Sibbick or Peter Moulson at the Department of Industry, Ashdown House, 123 Victoria Street, London SW1E 6RB (Telephone 01 212 0946 or 212 5892).

NB This guide was produced in March 1982. In October 1982 the Department of Industry published a 'general' licence for VANS which specifies conditions relating to the provision by companies of services using BT's networks.

Appendix B

Categories of EMS (as in User Survey)

This document refers to nine categories of EMS and illustrates what is meant by each category (NB 'see Price pp' refers to page numbers in the NCC publication *Introducing the Electronic Office* by S G Price, 1979).

1 *Communicating word processors* (see Price pp 43-45). This refers to transmission links between:

— identical models of communicating word processors;

— communicating word processors of different makes;

— a communicating word processor and another type of device (eg a mainframe computer, a telex machine, a phototypesetting machine).

2 *Facsimile systems* (see Price pp 46-52). This refers to the following types of document transmission:

— Group 1 (CCITT Recommendation T2); analogue (black, white and grey); 6 minutes (A4 page);

— Group 2 (CCITT Rec T3); analogue (black, white and grey); 3 minutes (A4 page);

— Group 3 (CCITT Draft Rec T4); digital (black and white only); 1 minute (A4 page);

— Group 4 (similar to Group 3, with error control techniques based on HDLC).

(See NCC publication *Introducing Data Communications Standards*, P R D Scott, 1979, pp 110-114.)

3 *Telex* (see Price pp 45-46). The term refers to:

— dial-up transmission over the Post Office public telex service to one of 90,000 other telex installations in the UK (1981 figures) or to one of a million telex installations worldwide;

— direct transmission between two or more points using teleprinters linked by private circuits.

(See *Introducing Data Communications Standards* pp 178-179.)

4 *Teletex* (see Price pp 66-69). A proposed new worldwide text-communication service, currently being defined by CCITT; sometimes, referred to as 'super-telex'.

(See *Introducing Data Communications Standards* p 177.)

5 *Private computer-based EMS* (see Price pp 56, 63-66). This refers to:

— private viewdata systems with message transfer facilities;

— private intra-organisation networks with EMS facilities developed by the organisation concerned (eg Texas Instruments, Bank of America);

— private intra-organisation networks with EMS facilities using suppliers' products (eg IBM Text Routeing System).

(See *Introducing Data Communications Standards* pp 181-182.)

6 *Public EMS* (see Price pp 54-66). This refers to:

— Prestel: closed user group facility;

— Prestel: enhanced to include message transfer facilities;

— Public switched telephone network (PSTN), PSS (the new packet switched service) and other public data networks;

— Value-added network services (VANS) provided by private organisations (where PTT policies permit), (eg TYMNET and TELENET).

7 *Simultaneous conferences* (see Price pp 69-70). This refers to systems which offer a substitute for travel to meetings, but require all members to be available at the same time, eg:

— voice conferencing (eg via private automatic branch exchanges (PABX), rented facilities);

— video conferencing (eg Confravision, snapshot);

— computer conferencing/screen sharing (eg Tymshare's AUG-MENT document preparation, distribution and filing system);

— computer-based voice conferencing (eg VMX);

— computer-based text conferencing (eg Notepad).

8 *Non-simultaneous (computer-based) conferencing* (see Price pp 70-73). This refers to systems which not only offer a substitute for travel to meetings, but also offer a substitute for the inconvenience of all members having to be available at the same time. Such systems are available on US VANS, (eg Tymshare's PLANET/FORUM system). Desirable features of such systems include:

— conferencing;

— messages;

— personal notebook;

— notice board.

9 *PABX* (see Price pp 73-76). This refers to private automatic branch telephone exchanges, eg:

— IBM 3750;

— Pye TMC's Herald;

— PO Monarch 120.

Appendix C

Categories of IMS

This document refers to nine categories of IMS and illustrates what is meant by each category (NB 'see Price pp' refers to page numbers in the NCC publication *Introducing the Electronic Office* by S G Price, 1979).

EXTERNAL INFORMATION

1 *Public information databases* (see Price pp 27, 52-56). These databases have been established to provide specific information, usually at a price, to anybody requiring it. Examples are:

— Prestel (UK Post Office) (NB see notes in items 3 and 4 below);

— Euronet-DIANE (Direct Information Access Network for Europe). This network, commissioned by the EEC, facilitates access by a wide range of users to European on-line information bases:

— Blaise (British Library Automated Information Service);

— GEISCO;

— Lockheed's Dialog;

— Dialtech;

— Info-line.

2 *External ad hoc computing services*. This refers to specialist timesharing computational services offering to paying organisations and individuals program libraries and computing power to provide help in solving one-off or out-of-the-ordinary problems such as financial

modelling, statistical analysis or engineering calculations. Examples are:

— IBM's Call 360;

— GEISCO.

(This does not refer to computing services for running standard company systems. Compare this with item 5 below.)

OPERATIONAL INFORMATION

3 *Staff access to the corporate database*. This refers to accesses by staff *requesting* information from the organisation's *corporate* database. At one level, an employee accesses that part of the database relevant to his particular job, at another level he is able to gain access to operational information about all aspects of the organisation's activities (subject to security restrictions). This does not refer to situations where employees are supplied regularly with batches of standard information. Examples of access techniques are:

— from a VDU into an on-line system;

— through a private viewdata system (or through the closed user group facility of Prestel);

— through the submission of a job to a batch processing system;

— from a telephone handset with recorded voice response output;

— *computer-based* indexing, cross-referencing and retrieval of information from the corporate database held on microfiche or microfilm (see Price pp 25-26, 80-81); compare this with item 6 below.

4 *Public access to the corporate database*. This refers to corporate operational data being made available for public inspection as part of the organisation's operations (eg bank account information, stock availability information) or to promote the organisation (eg promotional material, company accounts, company profiles). Prestel could be employed.

5 *Internal ad hoc computing services.* This refers to in-house services offering employees program libraries and computing power to provide help in solving one-off or out-of-the-ordinary problems such as financial modelling, statistical analysis or engineering calculations. This refers to an in-house alternative to item 2 above.

6 *Bulk storage of historical information* (see Price pp 25-26, 80-81). This refers to information which is no longer current and which is accessed infrequently. It is removed from day-to-day information management systems and stored by such means as microfiche or microfilm as hard copy, or on magnetic tape or other high volume computer storage media. Compare this with item 3 above, where the access is *computer-based;* here it is not.

ADMINISTRATIVE INFORMATION

7 *Administrative information systems.* This refers to systems for the access to and dissemination of administrative, as opposed to operational, information. The examples of access techniques given in item 3 above apply here also. Examples of administrative information are:

— telephone directories (eg colleagues, suppliers, customers);

— organisation charts;

— descriptions of job vacancies;

— company procedures;

— correspondence registers.

8 *Update of administrative information.* This refers to systems for the updating of administrative information, for example by word processors.

PERSONAL INFORMATION

9 *Personal information systems* (see Price p 14). This refers to systems which provide an electronic alternative to traditional manual methods of personal information management. Examples of personal information are:

— diaries;

— schedules of appointments;

— travel plans;

— lists of names, addresses and telephone and telex numbers;

— tickler files (a tickler file is one that serves as a reminder and which is arranged to bring matters to timely attention);

— miscellaneous files relating to work in progress.

Appendix D

Office Technology Sub-group: Objectives, Terms of Reference and Policy

OBJECTIVES

To advise on the policy and to plan and take the actions required to ensure the efficient and effective introduction of technology into the office. To ensure such introduction improves the Group's business communications.

TERMS OF REFERENCE

1 To ensure existing and new applications of office technology in the Group (UK and overseas) are monitored to consistent standards (in terms of technical performance, costs, benefits, compatibility, and social and organisational effects).

2 To ensure opportunities are taken to apply appropriate technology to the solution of information processing and communication problems already identified.

3 To promote evaluation in the group of new developments in office technology in order to establish whether it may be effectively applied.

4 To ensure surveys of information processing and communications needs are undertaken in the Group in order to identify opportunities for applications of office technology.

5 To co-ordinate implementation of technology such that opportunities to integrate individual applications into a coherent communications network are identified and exploited. To promote the concept of a communications network.

6   To develop and recommend methodology for efficient implementation of office technology.

7   To ensure research is undertaken to increase understanding of tasks and functions performed in offices and the social and organisational implications of change.

8   To ensure technical developments in office technology inside and outside the Group are kept under review.

9   To foster understanding of the technology and to help educate people at all appropriate levels in the Group about its application to office tasks and functions.

10 To keep Group Employee Relations and Group Training and Development Departments informed of developments and implications of new technology which may require action by those departments.

11 To keep under constant review developments in equipment for the office of the future and to advise the company on preferred suppliers.

12 To advise on the organisation and resources to execute the actions required.

POLICY

1   The Office Technology Sub-Group of the Systems Working Party is responsible for guiding the implementation of new office technology. It will develop competence to support user requirements and to appraise proposals.

2   The Office Technology Sub-Group will be informed of all major proposals for introducing new office technology in the Group so that developments may be effectively co-ordinated.

3   When introducing new office technology, particular attention should be given to consultation with, and involvement of, users. Developments are to comply with Group Personnel policy and relevant agreements, such as the Employment Agreement and Management Services Agreement in the UK.

4   Education and training programmes will be devised to meet the particular needs of departments introducing new systems and/or equipment, but the Sub-Group will also look for opportunities to develop greater understanding of the implications of technological change among Company managers and staff.

5   In order to ensure effective implementation of new technology, attention must be given to the design of appropriate office environments and systems.

6   The Sub-Group will guide users on preferred suppliers according to supplier evaluation criteria it has defined, which take into account the pace of technological change.

7   The Sub-Group will identify and promote evaluation of developments in office technology which are beyond the responsibility or resources of individual divisions or functions.

8   All implementations of new technology are subject to normal financial authorisation procedures.

9   In view of the differing technologies, their widespread application and their potential effects, the Sub-Group will ensure all implementations are monitored so that experience may be shared and directions reviewed. As much attention must be given to understanding and accommodating organisational and social change as to understanding technology.

10   The Sub-Group must ensure that the telecommunications capability of new office technology is recognised as fundamental to success, providing support for both formal and informal communications.

Appendix E

Glossary

AIM: Datapoint's Associative Index Method (for information storage and retrieval)

ARC: Datapoint's Attached Resource Computer local network

ASC: administrative support centre

BABT: British Approval Board for Telecommunications

BEAB: British Electro-technical Approvals Board

bit/s: bits per second

BLEND: Birmingham and Loughborough Electronic Network Development (an experimental electronic journal project funded by the British Library Research and Development Department)

blocking: a condition encountered on some PABXs used to switch a mix of voice and non-voice traffic in which it becomes impossible to connect a free inlet to a free outlet because no path can be found through the PABX; modern digital PABXs/data switches have been designed to be non-blocking

BSI: British Standards Institution

BT: British Telecom (the UK PTT with responsibilities defined in the British Telecommunications Act of 1981)

CAFS: content addressable file storage; also the name of an ICL product

Captain: Character and Pattern Telephone Access Information Network System (an experimental viewdata service provided in the Tokyo metropolitan area by NTT and the forerunner of a public national service in Japan)

CEC: Commission of the European Communities

CMOS: complementary metal oxide semi-conductor (chip technology)

Comet: an electronic mailbox service for text messages, which BL Systems Ltd have been licensed to operate

Dialcom: BT's electronic mail service, marketed by Telecom Gold Ltd (see Useful Addresses, item 1.1)

DISOSS: IBM's Distributed Office Support System

DoI: Department of Industry

DOSF: IBM's Distributed Office Support Facility

DPS: document preparation systems

EMS: electronic message systems (see also Appendix B)

enterprise union: a feature of Japanese industrial relations is the good worker-management relationship in large companies which is underpinned by the enterprise union (or company union), as opposed to the industry-wide union structure found in the UK

Euronet-DIANE: Direct Information Access Network for Europe (an important European external information service in which member countries of the European Community are collaborating)

FGCS: fifth-generation computer systems; also a JIPDEC project in Japan

Gateway: a software interface between a viewdata system and another computer system, eg an interface between BT's Prestel and a third party's computer system

Hermes:	a proposed electronic document viewing and delivery network for teletex terminals
I. M. P. :	OTL's Information Management Processor work-station
IMS:	information management systems (see also Appendix C)
INSIS:	Interinstitutional integrated Services Information System (an electronic office system which has been proposed for linking up European Community institutions, national ministries and parliaments)
IPSS:	International Packet Switched Service
ISDN:	Integrated Services Digital Network (to be provided by BT)
ISO:	International Organisation for Standardisation
ISX:	Datapoint's Information Switching Exchange
IT82:	Information Technology Year (1982) in the UK
Itecs:	Information Technology Centres
JIPDEC:	Japan Information Processing Development Centre
KIPS:	knowledge information processing systems
LAN:	local area network
Mbyte:	megabyte (ie one million bytes)
Mercury:	the first private network in the UK licensed to complete with BT
micron:	a unit of length equal to one-millionth of a metre
MPT:	managerial, professional and technical staff
ms:	millisecond
nemawashi:	a complex and socio-psychological form of inter-personal negotiation by which groups of Japanese employees reach a consensus

NMOS: N-channel metal oxide semi-conductor (chip technology)

NTT: Nippon Telegraph and Telephone Public Corporation (the Japanese PTT responsible for telecommunication services within Japan)

OA: office automation

OCR: optical character recognition

OMR: optical mark reader

opportunity hours: time which has been released by the use of new technology and which is now available to undertake additional useful activities

OTL: Office Technology Limited

PABX: private automatic branch exchange

PROFS: IBM's Professional Office System

PSS: BT's public packet switched service, also called SwitchStream 1, which began full commercial operation in August 1981

PSTN: BT's public switched telephone network

RAM: random access memory (ie having both read and write capability)

ROM: read only memory (cf RAM)

rigour: the strict adherence to rules; an organisation has creative thinkers and 'doers'; in between is a stratum of bureaucrats or 'rigour people' who work in inflexible ways with paperwork and procedures and to whom the system of communication between the thinkers and doers is of paramount importance; to rigour people form filling becomes an end in itself rather than a means to an end; the good news is that office automation will provide electronic systems for the more direct communication between thinkers and doers and release them from being subservient to the rigour people

secretariat: see ASC

SPC: stored program control (exchanges)

STAIRS: IBM's Information Storage and Retrieval System

STATUS: ICL's Information Storage and Retrieval System

tickler file: a personal file of prompts to remind the file holder of things requiring his attention

time compression: the use of new technology to reduce the time taken to carry out a particular function

ULSI: ultra large scale integration (chips)

VANS: value added network services (see also Appendix A)

VLSI: very large scale integration (chips)

VRS: Video Response System (an experimental interactive visual information system operated by NTT and available in Tokyo)

WCY83:   the United Nations World Communications Year (1983)

X-Stream: BT's new range of digital transmission services

Appendix F

Bibliography

1.1   *Introducing the Electronic Office,* S G Price, NCC Publications, 1979.

1.2   *Office Automation – The Report of a Survey of UK Users,* J A T Pritchard and P A Wilson, NCC report, 1980.

1.3   *Planning Office Automation – Electronic Message Systems,* J A T Pritchard and P A Wilson, NCC Publications, 1982.

1.4   *Information Management Systems – Strategic Issues and Design Considerations:* The Report of a Series of Workshops in 1981, J A T Pritchard and I Cole, NCC report, August 1981.

1.5   *Electronic Mail Systems – A Practical Evaluation Guide,* W J Welch and P A Wilson, NCC Publications, 1981.

1.6   *Facsimile Equipment – A Practical Evaluation Guide,* W J Welch and P A Wilson, NCC Publications, 1982.

1.7   *Viewdata Systems – A Practical Evaluation Guide,* R Firth, NCC Publications, 1982.

1.8   *Office System Printers – A Practical Evaluation Guide,* M A Condon, NCC Publications, 1982.

1.9   *Managers and the New Technology,* G B Bleazard and S G Price, Report and Executive Summary of a Multi-Client Study, 1981.

1.10 Is OA the Best Darned Thing You've Ever Seen? Maybe, Steven M Abraham, *Computerworld,* 28 September 1981, pp SR/21, 23 (NB this is part of *Computerworld's* 76-page special report on Office Automation).

1.11   *Office Technology Benefits,* P A Wilson and J A T Pritchard, NCC Publications, 1983.

2.1   Office of Future Seen Answer to Paper Blizzard, Nancy Finn, *Computerworld,* 28 September 1981, pp SR/71-72.

2.2   Europe and the New Information Technology – A Community Strategy for the 1980s, *NCC Interface Supplement,* December 1980.

       — The Microelectronics Industry in Europe, Christopher Layton, Director: High Technology, EEC Commission.

       — Microelectronics and Europe's Industrial Future, Viscount Etienne Davignon, EEC Commissioner for Industry.

       — Social Effects of the Technology, John Morley, Director: Employment Policy, EEC Commission.

       — Education and Training for Technology, Geoffrey Hubbard, Director: Council for Educational Technology for the United Kingdom.

2.3   *Information Resources Management: Concept and Cases,* Forest W Horton Jr, Association for Systems Management, Cleveland, Ohio, 1979.

2.4   *Looking for an Exciting Career in a Wide Open Field? How About Considering Information Science?,* American Society for Information Science, Washington DC.

4.1   *Personal Documentation for Professionals: Means and Methods,* V Stibic, North Holland Publishing Company, 1980.

4.2   *NCC Survey of On-line Information Systems,* NCC Information Services, 1981.

4.3   *Directory of On-line Databases,* R Landau *et al.* Vol. 2, No. 1, Autumn 1980, (ISSN 0913-6840), Cuadra Associates Inc (see Useful Addresses, item 4.2).

4.4   *On-line Bibliographic Databases,* J L Hall and M J Brown, Second edition, (ISBN 08103-05283), Aslib Publications Sales, 1981 (see Useful Addresses, item 4.3).

4.5   Picture Prestel – the 'How' and the 'When', Keith Clarke, *Viewdata and TV User,* July 1980, pp 22-23, 25.

4.6   Retrieving Information, V A J Maller, *Datamation,* September 1980, pp 164, 166, 168-170, 172.

4.7   CAFS – A Pace-making Product that's Storing up Marketing Headaches, Philip Hunter, *Computer Weekly,* 4 March 1982, p 18.

4.8   Rival to CAFS is Backed by UK Merchant Banks, Rory Johnston, *Computer Weekly,* 10 September 1981, pp 1, 48.

4.9   Key Role Emerges for IBM 8100 Comms Processor, Boris Sedacca, *Computer Weekly,* 7 January 1982, p 2.

4.10   *Friends Provident Life Office,* UK Form 24-8102, IBM (UK) Ltd.

4.11   An Office Communications System, G H Engel, J Groppuso, R A Lowenstein and W G Traub, *IBM Systems Journal,* Vol 18, No 3, 1979, pp 402-431.

4.12   A Research Perspective on Computer-Assisted Office Work, A M Gruhn and A C Hohl, *IBM Systems Journal,* Vol 18, No 3, 1979, pp 432-456.

4.13   A System for the Automated Office Environment, P C Gardner Jr., *IBM Systems Journal,* Vol 20, No 3, 1981, pp 321-345.

5.1   Integrated Systems Bid for Key Role in Automated Office, William A Saxton and Morris Edwards, *Canadian Data-systems,* July 1980, pp 86-87.

5.2   The Office Supercontroller – Next Step in the Electronic Office, Dan Hosage, *Telecommunications* (Euro-Global Edition), December 1980, pp 23-27.1.

5.3   Telecommunications Strategies for Office Automation, Thomas A McWalters and Sheldon L Brill, *Telecommunications* (Euro-Global Edition), December 1980, pp 56-58.

5.4   *The Datapoint ISX (Information Switching Exchange) Information Leaflet,* Datapoint Corporation.

5.5   *C & C Office Systems – NEC Office Automation,* Nippon Electric Company Limited, Publication E01021.

5.6   *The Plessey Strategy for Business Communications in the Electronic 80s,* Plessey Office Systems Limited, Publication No: 7921.

5.7   Managers Hedge their Bets, Chris Barnard, *Computing Europe*, 26 November 1981, p 23.

5.8   Tying Together the UK Nets, Chris Youett, *Computing Europe*, 26 November 1981, p 35.

5.9   The Lure of Voice and Data, Margaret Coffey, *Computing Europe*, 26 November 1981, p 37.

5.10   Comms: Key to Productivity, Margaret Coffey, *Computing Europe*, 21 January 1982, p 19.

5.11   The PBX: Today and Tomorrow (Part 1), George Stubbs and Anthony Pastelis, *Telecommunications* (Global Edition), February 1982, pp 17-20, 22, 66.

5.12   How to Prepare for the Coming Changes, *EDP Analyzer*, April 1979.

5.13   How to Use Advanced Technology, *EDP Analyzer*, September 1979.

5.14   How Companies are Preparing for Change, *EDP Analyzer*, February 1980.

5.15   Introducing Advanced Technology, *EDP Analyzer*, March 1980.

5.16   Educating Executives on New Technology, *EDP Analyzer*, November 1980.

5.17   The Coming Impact of New Technology, *EDP Analyzer*, January 1981.

5.18   The Challenge of 'Increased Productivity', *EDP Analyzer*, April 1981.

5.19   Practical Office Automation, *EDP Analyzer*, January 1982.

5.20   How to Boost Your Office Productivity, Wayne L Rhodes Jr., *Infosystems*, 8/80, pp 38-40, 42.

5.21   *District Councils Review*, March 1982, p 77.

5.22   Crisis in the Workplace – Selling the Staff on Office Automation, Carol T Gaffney, *Computerworld*, 28 September 1981, p SR 11.

5.23   Success of Office Automation Depends on User Acceptance, Not High Technology, Ursula Connor, *Computerworld*, 28 September 1981, pp SR 46-47.

5.24   Workers said Fearful of 'Creeping Automation', J Thomas Horrigan, *Computerworld*, 28 September 1981, p SR 68.

5.25   *Office Technology: The Trade Union Response – First Report of the APEX Word Processing Working Party*, Association of Professional, Executive, Clerical and Computer Staff (APEX), March 1979; (see Useful Addresses, item 5.1).

5.26   *Automation and the Office Worker – Report of Office Technology Working Party*, Association of Professional, Executive, Clerical and Computer Staff (APEX), March 1980.

5.27   *Microtechnology – A Programme for Action*, Banking Insurance & Finance Union (BIFU), (see Useful Addresses, item 5.2).

5.28   DoI Staff Stall on Technology, Claire O'Grady, *Computing Europe*, 26 November 1981, p 1.

5.29   Civil Service Unions Pose IT82 Threat, *Computing Europe*, 28 January 1982, p 2.

5.30   Civil Service to Agree Job Deal, Sarah Underwood, *Computing Europe*, 18 March 1982, p 3.

5.31   BIFU Seeks Technology Agreement, *Computing Europe*, 18 March 1982, p 2.

5.32   Unions Approve, *Computer Weekly*, 25 March 1982, p 1.

5.33   *New Technology – An Interim Agreement*, SCPS document A.8/82, 25 March 1982; (see Useful Addresses, item 5.3).

6.1   *Designing Systems for People*, L Damodaran, A Simpson and P A Wilson, NCC Publications, 1980.

6.2   *Designing Systems for People*, No. 67 NCC Guidelines for Computing Management, October 1981.

6.3   *Security in On-line Systems*, J A T Pritchard, NCC Publications, 1979.

6.4   *Computer Security: Security Software*, J A T Pritchard, NCC Publications, 1980.

6.5   Safeguarding the Individual, Janice Wright, *Computing Europe*, 4 March 1982, p 28.

6.6   *A Draft Data Protection Code of Practice for Systems Containing a*

Word Processor, H H W Pitcher, NCC, Reference HPo31A, 21 November 1980.

6.7   *Data Protection – The Government's Proposals for Legislation*, Cmnd. 8539, HMSO, April 1982.

6.8   *Data Encryption*, J A T Pritchard, NCC Publications, 1980.

6.9   The Golden Star on the DP Horizon, Chris Barnard, *Computing Europe*, 19 November 1981, p 26.

6.10 Watching the Human Factor, Margaret Coffey, *Computing Europe*, 4 February 1982, p 20.

6.11 Voice Input/Output – Special Report, *Computing Europe*, 4 March 1982, pp 18-27.

6.12 Guides to Computing Standards series, (a series of reference documents for standards for computing and office automation), NCC Standardisation Office:

   — No. 1: *The Making of Standards*, R M O'Connor (September 1981).

   — No. 10: *Automation in Bibliography*, A Hopkinson (November 1980).

   — No. 17: *Keyboard Layouts*, H McGregor Ross (November 1980).

   — No. 20: *Microfilm and Microfiche*, K Oldham (November 1980).

6.13 Putting Interests of Suppliers First, Paul Malvern, *Computing Europe*, 26 November 1981, p 32.

6.14 The Systems Interconnection Standard Nears Completion, Frank Taylor, *Computer Weekly*, 4 February 1982, p 15.

6.15 Users Need A Clear Victor on Standards, Steve Connor, *Computing Europe*, 26 November 1981, p 33.

6.16 Ethernet Close to US Standard Acceptance, Donald Kennett, *Computer Weekly*, 11 March 1982, p 7.

6.17 LAN Suppliers Fight for 'Standard' Status, *Computer Weekly*, 18 March 1982, pp 25, 28.

6.18 A T & T Brake on Standard for Viewdata, Donald Kennett, *Computer Weekly,* 22 October 1981, p 1.

7.1 Baker Lashes Government for DP Failure, *Computing Europe,* 17 December 1981, p 6.

7.2 State Makes Hollow Noises about IT82, *Computing Europe,* 7 January 1982, p 11.

7.3 Baker's Strategy Flounders, Liz Else and Helena Sturridge, *Computing Europe,* 7 January 1982, p 16.

7.4 Call for Better Planning, *Computer Weekly,* 12 November 1981, p 7.

7.5 IT Must Depend on Private Enterprise, says Minister, Robert Parry, *Computer Weekly,* 11 February 1982, p 1.

7.6 *Policy for the UK Electronics Industry,* Electronics Economic Development Committee (EDC) report, April 1982, (published by NEDO, see Useful Addresses, item 7.1).

7.7 *Adapting to the Information Society,* National Electronics Council Report, March 1981, (see Useful Addresses, item 7.2).

7.8 Ten Companies Join the Race to Produce 256,000-bit Chips, Kevin Cahill, *Computer Weekly,* 25 February 1982, p 8.

7.9 The International Break-away Effort, Isabel Gouveia Lima, *Computing Europe,* 29 October 1982, pp 22-23.

7.10 National Strategy is Boosting Japan into Fifth-Generation, Kevin Cahill, *Computer Weekly,* 25 February 1982, p 10.

7.11 Human Brain is the Pattern for Japan's Futuristic System, Kevin Cahill, *Computer Weekly,* 4 March 1982, p 12.

7.12 *Proceedings of the International Conference on Fifth-Generation Computer Systems (FGCS),* October 19-22, 1981, published by JIPDEC, Tokyo.

7.13 UK Focuses on Japan's 5th-Generation Vision (editorial), *Computing Europe,* 11 February 1982, p 17.

7.14 UK Earmarks £250M for 5th-Generation Kit, Rex Malik, *Computing Europe,* 18 February 1982, p 1.

7.15   UK Plots Fifth-Generation, Rex Malik, *Computing Europe*, 25 February 1982, p 14.

7.16   UK Fifth-Generation Cash in Doubt, Boris Sedacca, *Computer Weekly*, 25 February 1982, p 1.

7.17   Govt Sets up Fifth-Generation Study, Boris Sedacca, *Computer Weekly*, 15 April 1982, p 1.

Appendix G

Useful Addresses

1.1 Telecom Gold Ltd
Automated Office Services
42 Weston Street
London SE1 3QD
(Telephone: 01-403-6777)

4.1 Enquiry Desk
Information Department
The National Computing Centre Ltd
Oxford Road
Manchester M1 7ED
(Telephone: 061-228-6333)
(Telex: 668962)
(NB The Enquiry Desk's telephone is manned between the hours of
10 am to 12 am and from 2 pm to 4 pm)

4.2 Cuadra Associates Inc.
1523 Sixth Street, Suite 12
Santa Monica
California 90401
USA
(Telephone: (213) 451-0644)

4.3 Aslib Publications Sales
3 Belgrave Square
London SW1X 8PL

4.4 Euronet-DIANE
B.P. 777
Luxembourg
(for free copy of pocket directory)

4.5   Datastar Marketing
      199 High Street
      Orpington BR6 0PF
      (Telephone: 0689-38488)

4.6   Euronet-DIANE News
      Published by:
      Directorate General for Information Market and Innovation
      Euronet-DIANE Information
      Jean Monnet Building, B4 009
      Commission of the European Communities (CEC)
      1615 Luxembourg (Grand Duchy)
      (Telephone: (352) 4301 3020 (and 2879 Ansaphone))
      (Telex: 2752 EURDOC LU)

4.7   Computel Ltd
      Eastern Road
      Bracknell
      Berkshire
      (Telephone: 0344-26767)
      (Telex: 848625)

4.8   Networks Marketing
      British Telecom
      Freepost
      London EC4B 4TS   (no postage stamp is required)

4.9   The British Telecom Film Library
      25 The Burroughs
      Hendon
      London NW4 4AT
      (Telephone: 01-202-5342)

5.1   Association of Professional, Executive, Clerical & Computer Staff
      (APEX)
      22 Worple Road
      Wimbledon
      London SW19 4DF
      (Telephone: 01-947-3131/6)

5.2 Banking Insurance & Finance Union (BIFU)
Sheffield House
Portsmouth Road
Esher
Surrey KT10 9BH
(Telephone: Esher: 0372-66624/66412/66422)

5.3 Society of Civil & Public Servants (SCPS)
124-130 Southwark Street
London SE1 0TU
(Telephone: 01-928-9671)

6.1 Dept M12
BSI Sales
101 Pentonville Road
London N1 9ND
(Telephone: 01-837-8801)

7.1 National Economic Development Office
Millbank Tower
Millbank
London SW1P 4QX
(Telephone: 01-211-3352 or 4717)

7.2 National Electronics Council Report *Adapting to the Information Society*
Contact:
Abell House
John Islip Street
London SW1

7.3 JIPDEC (Japan Information Processing Development Centre)
3-5-8 Shibakoen
Minatu-ku
Tokyo 105
Japan

Appendix H

Index